do life

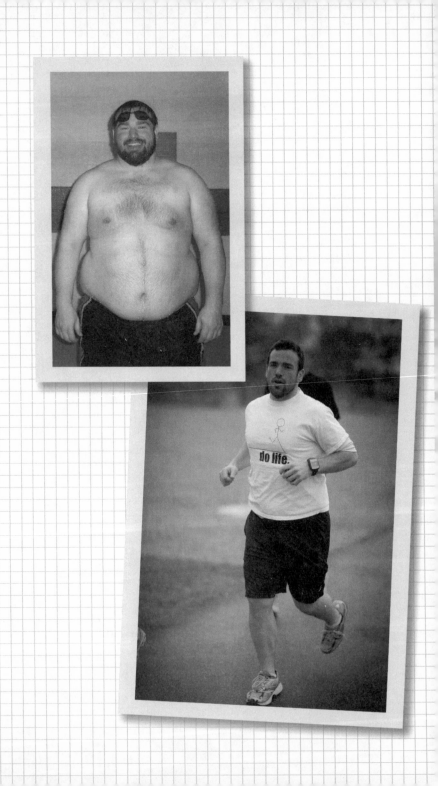

do life

The Creator of

MY 120-POUND JOURNEY

Shows How to Run Better,

Go Farther, and

Find Happiness

BEN DAVIS

NEW AMERICAN LIBRARY

NEW AMERICAN LIBRARY
Published by New American Library, a division of
Penguin Group (USA) Inc., 375 Hudson Street,
New York, New York 10014, USA
Penguin Group (Canada), 90 Eglinton Avenue East, Suite 700, Toronto,
Ontario M4P 2Y3, Canada (a division of Pearson Penguin Canada Inc.)
Penguin Books Ltd., 80 Strand, London WC2R 0RL, England
Penguin Ireland, 25 St. Stephen's Green, Dublin 2,
Ireland (a division of Penguin Books Ltd.)
Penguin Group (Australia), 250 Camberwell Road, Camberwell, Victoria 3124,
Australia (a division of Pearson Australia Group Pty. Ltd.)
Penguin Books India Pvt. Ltd., 11 Community Centre, Panchsheel Park,
New Delhi - 110 017, India
Penguin Group (NZ), 67 Apollo Drive, Rosedale, Auckland 0632,
New Zealand (a division of Pearson New Zealand Ltd.)
Penguin Books (South Africa) (Pty.) Ltd., 24 Sturdee Avenue,
Rosebank, Johannesburg 2196, South Africa

Penguin Books Ltd., Registered Offices:
80 Strand, London WC2R 0RL, England

Published by New American Library,
a division of Penguin Group (USA) Inc.

First Printing, January 2013
10 9 8 7 6 5 4 3 2 1

▉ REGISTERED TRADEMARK—MARCA REGISTRADA

LIBRARY OF CONGRESS CATALOGING-IN-PUBLICATION DATA:

Davis, Ben.
Do life: the creator of my 120-pound journey shows how to run better,
go farther, and find happiness/Ben Davis.
p. cm.
ISBN 978-0-451-41491-5
1. Marathon running—Training. 2. Ironman triathlons. I. Title.
GV1065.17.T73D38 2013
796.42'52—dc23
                              2012027815

Set in ITC New Baskerville Std
Designed by Pauline Neuwirth

Printed in the United States of America

PUBLISHER'S NOTE
Outdoor recreational activities are by their very nature potentially hazardous. All participants in
such activities must assume the responsibility for their own actions and safety. If you have any health
problems or medical conditions, consult with your physician before undertaking any outdoor activities.
The information contained in this guidebook cannot replace sound judgment and good decision
making, which can help reduce risk exposure, nor does the scope of this book allow for disclosure of all
the potential hazards and risks involved in such activities. Learn as much as possible about the outdoor
recreational activities in which you participate, prepare for the unexpected, and be cautious. The
reward will be a safer and more enjoyable experience.
     The recipes contained in this book are to be followed exactly as written. The publisher is not
responsible for your specific health or allergy needs that may require medical supervision. The
publisher is not responsible for any adverse reactions to the recipes contained in this book.
     While the author has made every effort to provide accurate telephone numbers, Internet addresses
and other contact information at the time of publication, neither the publisher nor the author assumes
any responsibility for errors, or for changes that occur after publication. Further, publisher does not
have any control over and does not assume any responsibility for author or third-party Web sites or their
content.

To Meemaw, for encouraging me to find a little happiness

contents

do life

foreword

YOU NEVER KNOW when you might be struck with a little inspiration.

A year ago my husband sent me a video on YouTube. It was the story of Ben Davis and the journey he had taken over the past two years of his life. His story deeply touched me. I literally had goose bumps and tears streaming down my face as I watched his video. Ben hasn't had the easiest life. Weighing in at 365 pounds, he felt depressed and defeated. He wasn't happy. He was drowning as his life slipped away.

The remarkable thing about Ben is that he found the courage to face his fears and found the power to take control of his life. He started to fight. He didn't have any gimmicks, any quick fixes; he just got out there and started running. The simple act of moving one foot in front of the other started to give Ben hope. He started to go a little farther and a little farther until he was ready to run a 5K. Then came a 10K, a half marathon, and eventually a marathon. Ben has even done something I only dream about: He has completed an Ironman. Two Ironmans. Ben took himself from helplessness to living life to the fullest.

We all have fears in life. My fears are about not being a good mother, wife, and athlete. I recently went through a time in my career where I realized I wasn't happy. I was just going though the motions, but not living. After months of making excuses, I finally had to face my fears and find another coach. It was extremely stressful, but the journey was well worth it.

What finally gave me the inspiration to make the change? People like Ben Davis. Ordinary people doing miraculous things—this is what Ben is about. If he could find the courage to start a journey that would be painful, emotionally exhausting, and extremely long, then why I was hiding from my fears? Ben's journey was much more difficult than mine and he found the strength to start. I knew I had to start my own.

If you look up the word *inspire* in the dictionary, you'll find it says "prompt to extraordinary actions." Ben found the prompt to change his life. A little inspiration led to him taking control and gaining a life that was passing him by. He is just an average guy who decided to take the road less traveled. He chose living over safe and comfortable. I hope that you can find the inspiration you are looking for in him. I hope it leads to "extraordinary actions" for all of you. I know it did for me. Three months after finding the courage to seek out a new coach, I made the 2012 Olympic Marathon team.

Ben inspired me. How will he inspire you?

—Kara Goucher

introduction

I'**M ASKED QUITE** often what keeps me going. What keeps me running, what makes me want to eat healthy foods, what makes me want to run five, ten, sometimes twenty miles? Why would I want to put myself through that, for lack of a better word, agony? The simple answer is that it's worth it. I made a decision four years ago to get a grip on my life. To take control. I called it "doing life." But what did that mean?

I certainly didn't always know the answer. For the vast majority of my life, I suffered from a crippling food addiction that led me into a downward spiral of depression, overeating, self-hatred, and eventually morbid obesity. It left me feeling lonely, empty, and sad, and I slowly began to isolate myself so that nobody would see what I had become. My relationships suffered. My girlfriend left me. I hid from and lied to the few friends I had left. But mostly, I lied to myself. It hurt too much to face the truth, and I settled into a sense of despair as my entire life disintegrated along with my health.

I was lucky. There were still people who loved me enough to shake me out of my stubborn denial and insistence that everything was "fine." When forced to face the hard truth, I decided to try a different way of life, something new and tentative and scary. Little by little, I realized that life didn't have to be this way, and that it certainly wasn't meant to be. I reached out to others and gradually reconnected. I stumbled at first, kept working at it, found my stride, and then I ran with it. And I ran as far as I could.

In less than two years, I went from weighing over 350 pounds and living a depressed, lonely, and completely sedentary lifestyle to officially becoming an Ironman, and I did it with my brother and father beside me. Now I am 130 pounds lighter and happier than I've ever been in my life. In those two years, I took action, jumped into a new lifestyle, and as a result I broke out of the cycle of depressed thoughts and actions that had been holding me back for years.

At first, Doing Life meant going public, allowing others in, and sharing my journey with the people who loved me. I never imagined how public that journey would ultimately become. Now Doing Life means living it to the fullest— getting off the couch and out of your head, finding something that inspires you, something that makes you smile, and something that helps you share that smile with the rest of the world.

Today, I spend my time traveling around the country, running with people I've never met before, hearing their stories, and speaking to groups about how I made such a big change in my life. Since deciding to Do Life, I've gone from barely going through the motions in solitude to living a full life out in the open—a life that I never could have imagined. I never knew that a life like this was out there waiting for me all along. And it's right there waiting for you, too.

This book is about running, sure, but it's also about life. It's the story of how I learned to do life when I fell in love with running. I hope it inspires you to run, whether it's just for fun, to lose weight, or to completely change your life. The chapters represent steps in a journey—mine, and possibly yours, too—out of the darkness and into the light, from barely slogging by to pushing yourself to the limits in all aspects of life. I found that light by running, and maybe you will, too. But running is a metaphor for life itself, and the lessons in this book will broadly apply. Maybe you're already running, and you want to run farther, or better. I'll teach you how to do that, too. There is no mystery, no secret ingredient that will take you from where you are today to the life you most want to live. All you need is a little bit of inspiration and the belief that it's possible. I hope that is exactly what I can give you.

I'll start at the beginning, in my darkest moments before deciding to turn my life around, and lead you through each step of the way, from facing the truth to jumping in, taking the occasional step backward, and pushing myself to the limit. This is my story, and yours may be completely different. Some of you will relate to the highs and the lows, and others of you have never been nearly that low. Either way, I'll do my best to help you write your own story as I tell you mine.

The Do Life movement is characterized by openness, accountability, and community. In that spirit, each chapter includes inspiring stories from my readers, as well as my answers to some of my most common reader questions. I'm also including tips, terms, and running guides for each type of race that I've covered, as well as a Running Glossary at the end of the book.

You now have everything that you need to take this moment, grab life, and get going. So, what are you waiting for? The rest of your life starts now. Let's do it.

going through the motions

*h*OW DID I *get here?*

This is a question that most people have asked themselves at some point in their lives, and I bet you have, too. Maybe you looked in the mirror and noticed a few extra pounds that you didn't remember accumulating, or found yourself in the gym for the first time in a while, barely able to finish what used to be an easy workout. If you're like me, maybe you avoided mirrors, passed up social invitations, and ignored the scale before ever realizing that your weight had gotten completely out of control.

Maybe you've never been to a dark place like the one I spent most of my life in. If you're on the right path, it's because your positive thoughts have encouraged you to take healthy actions, and vice versa. You believe that you deserve to be happy and healthy, and so you treat your mind and body well. You take healthy actions—like running, they make you feel good about yourself—and so you keep going.

If you haven't been making the best choices for your health or happiness, then you're most likely stuck in a vicious cycle of bad thoughts that inspired poor decisions. Those poor decisions made you think even worse thoughts, and those thoughts promoted more negative actions. Maybe you told yourself that you'd look ridiculous running around a track at your weight, and so you never started running or exercising. Not exercising led you to gain more weight, and that excess weight made you feel so embarrassed about the way you look that you don't want to even be seen in public. Thoughts and actions—those are the two things that get us into a bad place, and they're the same two things that can get us out.

Let me be clear—your "here" is probably different from mine. In fact, "here" is kind of like what they say about snowflakes—no two are exactly the same. Like I said, you might have a completely different problem than me, one with drugs or alcohol or an abusive relationship, or you might have a similar, weight-related one. You might not have a problem at all. Maybe you're just looking for a little inspiration to help kick-start your running. Either way, your exact cycles, and especially your thoughts, are specific to you, but it's always the simple matter of taking action that will change them.

The action I took was simple—I ran. Before that, the negative cycle that I was stuck in was always about my weight and my self-esteem. I've never been very confident, and the bigger I got, the worse I felt about myself. Feeling bad about myself caused me to overeat, make bad choices, gain weight, and then feel even worse about myself. It sounds so simple, doesn't it? Change one thing—a thought or an action—and your life will completely turn around.

When you spend as many years as I did being obese, your self-esteem suffers tremendously, making it nearly impossible to find the confidence to turn things around. But it wasn't always that way. In fact, throughout my childhood I felt mostly fine about myself. I was big, sure, but I was just another kid. It wasn't until the fifth grade that I even realized there was something different about me.

Of course, the one to clue me in to my "otherness" was a girl. Amanda Gray. Amanda was *the* hottest girl in fifth grade, probably in sixth grade, too, if you combined them. Up until this point in my life, I was known as the class clown, the kid who tried to make people laugh, got in trouble for talking too much, and was always trying to get a rise of out his teachers and classmates—the funny one.

I woke up one day in the middle of the school year feeling a little bit fed up with just being the funny one. I realized that I wanted to get the girl, but not just any girl—Amanda Gray would be mine. And why not? I would go from being the class clown to the popular guy who got the girl, and it would change my life for the better. I was certain that this would be the most exciting day of my young life.

I got myself psyched up and gathered as much confidence as I could. My family (my mother and father, my older brother, Jed, me, and my younger sister, Laura) lived in the middle of Beebe, Arkansas—"Your Dream Hometown." We lived close enough to school that I could walk, so I headed out early that morning. I sat down in our homeroom—Mr. Gorbet's first-period math class. I never was very good at math, but on that day I was ecstatic to be there.

I got out my pen and paper, and as simply as I could, in the neatest possible cursive that I could summon with my anxiously shaking hand, I wrote:

> Amanda, will you be my girlfriend? Circle yes or circle no.
>
> Sincerely, Ben

I handed it to my best friend, Scott, who delivered it to Amanda's best friend, Jennifer, who then passed it to Amanda. My heart pounded as I watched the note float across the room. I watched her closely as she received the slip of paper. I held my breath as she read it and I studied her reaction, searching for a clue. Luckily, she wasted no time in finding me before the bell rang and quickly put me out of my misery. She sat down across the desk from me. My heart was beating through my chest as I awaited her answer.

"Ben, I like you. . . . You're funny," she said. "But"—she paused dramatically—"you're too fat."

I felt like I had been kicked right in the gut, not that I wanted to think about my gut at that moment. I wished she had simply circled "no" and sent the note back. Instead, she said those words so matter-of-factly, as if it was to be expected that I was just too fat for her to be my girlfriend. I tried to laugh it off, but the truth is that I was deeply hurt. It wasn't just being called fat that hurt so much. It was the fact that, for the first time in my life, I realized that I was different. I wasn't just the funny guy; I was the big guy. I was the fat guy, and everyone else already knew it.

This was the life-altering moment when I became aware of my size. I was the biggest kid in fifth grade. I was the biggest kid in sixth grade, too, if you combined them. Deep down, I already knew this, but I hadn't accepted it or allowed it to make me feel like I was any different from the other kids. Instead, I had tried to joke and make fun of myself as a defense mechanism. I now realize that it was my way of distracting people from realizing how big I was. Heck, it even prevented *me* from realizing how big I was.

Of course, I now know how common it is for overweight people to use humor as a shield to protect themselves from being bullied or made fun of. At the time, I didn't realize any of this, but with Amanda's rejection, I had to finally be honest with myself. I was obese. I was different. There was something wrong with me.

But even knowing that there was a problem wasn't enough to convince me to solve it, and that's because it takes much more than knowing that there's a problem to turn it around. It takes courage and conviction, and most of all, confidence. You need to believe that you *deserve* to be better in order to start doing better, but as an obese fifth grader, I didn't have the maturity, mental fortitude, or belief in myself to do anything about my weight. I simply continued going through the motions. No matter how much it hurt or how insecure I felt, I just got through the days. I made light of my weight situation and continued to be the funny one who was often a punch line and a joke myself, never the hero who got the girl or saved the day.

As you can easily guess, my weight spiraled further out of control in the years after Amanda Gray crushed my heart. Soon, I didn't just feel different from everyone else, but I was trapped in a terrible cycle of overeating, laziness, and self-loathing. Before I could even ask myself how I got there, I was no longer just a chunky kid but a morbidly obese teenager. Even a simple doctor's appointment for strep throat had turned into a conversation about the health risks that I was facing if I didn't make a drastic change soon.

"Ben, in the end, all it comes down to is one thing," he said. "Your dad is going to outlive you if you keep living like this."

Like this.

It wasn't hard to figure out what he meant by "this." In those days, I sat alone in front of a computer screen playing video games for eighteen hours a day. I placed little importance on my relationships with my family. I didn't place

much importance on anything, but the lack of a familial bond was glaring. The truth is that I was jealous of the bonds my other family members shared, but I never made an effort because of my apathy toward anything and everything.

My sister and mom were always together. My sister is handicapped, so she was pretty dependent on my mom growing up; plus they were the only girls in the family. My dad and brother had more in common and spent their days training for and planning adventure races together, heading out into the wilderness every so often with a set of coordinates and spending the next twenty-four to thirty-six hours searching for checkpoints in the woods over hundreds of miles. I was always envious when they would load up and head off together for a weekend—jealous not only of the time they were spending together, but also of the fact that they weren't physically incapable of doing this sort of thing like I was.

I was the awkward middle kid with a weight problem and an Internet addiction. My mom owned a restaurant, so I got all the free greasy food that a teenager could possibly dream of. The rest of the time, I ate pizza for every meal. Just a year before, my friend Preston and I had decided to start a pizza box collection. "Think about it," he said. "We eat, like, five pizzas every week. If we just hang on to the boxes, eventually we'll hold the world record for the biggest pizza box collection."

We dedicated the next two years or so to the cause, and we were very successful. My bedroom served as the storing house for our collection, and soon it was filled with all kinds of pizza boxes—big pizza boxes, small pizza boxes, medium pizza boxes, pizza boxes from Washington, D.C., pizza boxes from Boston, and pizza boxes from Tennessee. A few of the pizza boxes were donated to us from friends and family members, but the majority of the boxes we emptied ourselves. To be honest, I emptied most of them by myself.

At the same time that the doctor was talking to me about the health risks associated with living "like this," my bedroom contained 974 pizza boxes. Even Preston had lost interest in our collection at that point. In retrospect, I realize that I must have been the only person who wasn't completely disturbed by my bizarre collection. The collection had become a creative way for me to justify my debilitating food addiction. It was as if I was building a monument to my obesity that existed outside of my own body.

So, for me, figuring out what it meant to live "like this" was easy. For you, it might be different. If you know that you're on the wrong track, you need to figure out exactly what is holding you back from embracing life and doing life to the fullest. Like me, you probably already know deep down where the problem lies. I knew it starting in fifth grade, but it took many more years for me to take action and start running.

Even if things aren't as severe for you as they were for me back then, there's always room for improvement. I still struggle every day to keep my boat afloat, to run as much as I should, and eat as little as I should. So, tell me. Tell yourself—what is holding you back? What do you turn to when you're feeling down? What behavior, addiction, or habit makes you feel a little uncomfortable or ill at ease? Is it food? Alcohol? Drugs? Something else entirely? Is it not one specific thing, but more of a way of life? Are you just stuck in a rut of depression and loneliness, unable to leave the house but desperate for human contact and camaraderie?

It's very possible that it's more than one thing. Those negative cycles between our thoughts and actions can be tricky. Just when we think we've nailed down the problem, another one often rears its ugly head. "I'll start a new running regime tomorrow," you tell yourself, and then the next

day you pick up a pack of cigarettes. "I'll leave this dead-end relationship," you decide, and then you let your training slide and end up feeling even more worthless. But no matter what "living like this" means for you, if you know that there's a problem, it's time to stop. It's time to acknowledge it, look it in the face, and replace it with positive thoughts and positive actions that will help you start really living or doing life.

Hearing the doctor's warnings back in high school was shocking. Obviously, "this" was no way to live, but just as I did in fifth grade, I ignored it. One day I would get my life together, I told myself, but not now. I mean, Diablo (the Lord of Terror) wasn't very well going to annihilate himself and save the wonderful people of Tristram. Besides, there was too much cereal to eat . . . too many *Saved by the Bell* reruns to watch. And, as much as I hated to admit it, my weight had gotten too far out of control. It was overwhelming and I couldn't even begin to think about how to tackle a task as big as completely changing my life.

Everything we do is a choice—every action, every thought, every feeling. We choose every day whether to feel apathetic or passionate, lazy or inspired, and the easy choice is often not the one that is best for us. Denial is easy. Inaction is easy. Selfishness, excuses, and indifference are easy. Honesty, positivity, and action, on the other hand, take bravery. Back then, I wasn't brave. I made the easy choice: denial. I turned from my problems and simply looked the other way.

When you live in a place of denial, things can only get worse, not better. This is one way that you can recognize exactly where you are in this process. Do you feel like things are getting better? Do you feel in control of your life? Do you have something positive to turn to every time you feel down? Now, when I've had a bad day or start feeling sluggish, I go for a run, but back then, I relied on negative and harmful behaviors to help me get by.

Remember, every single person is somewhere along this same path, no matter how functional or dysfunctional you may seem. Running took me from being extremely unhealthy to having far fewer problems, emotionally and physically, but that doesn't mean that I'm perfectly healed. Maybe your situation is grim, or perhaps you're on the other end of the spectrum. Either way, it's always a good idea to check in with yourself from time to time to make sure that your thoughts and actions are taking you down a healthy path.

A huge clue that will help you figure out where you're going wrong is to look at the things that you're doing in secret. Keeping secrets and hiding certain behaviors from the people around you are sure signs that these actions are dragging you down. Do you sneak a cigarette in secret when you're feeling stressed or down a quick shot when nobody's looking? I am prone to indulging in "secret eating," often in the form of sugary cereal in the middle of the night. No matter how far I've come, I'm still tempted to sneak into the kitchen when everyone else is asleep. We do these things in private because we're ashamed, and it only makes sense that in order to fully live our lives we need to discontinue the behaviors that we're ashamed of.

By the time I was in college, I was still choosing denial. Everywhere I turned, I saw some reminder of the person I had let myself become. In turn, I had to fight a constant battle to push it out of my mind. I decided that if I didn't face my problems, then they simply didn't exist. I avoided mirrors, I stopped wearing my seat belt because it was too tight, and I had to turn sideways to take a shower because I couldn't fit in a normal position. My weight continued its climb. Three hundred ten became 320, then 330, 340, and ultimately 350.

Eventually, even denial wasn't easy anymore. Everything was hard. Everything was sad. Halfhearted attempts to lose weight peppered my collegiate career, but none gained traction. The cycle was vicious and oppressive. Lose some weight and gain more, again and again and again. I thought that I was trying everything, that I was doing everything "right." After all, we all know exactly what it takes to lose weight— eat fewer calories than you burn. But if it were as simple as that, none of us would be overweight, would we? The problem is that those "diet plans" lack a cure for the emotional component, the insecurities and self-hatred that make us doubt ourselves, tell ourselves that we don't deserve to succeed and could never do it.

Sure, I went through the motions of dieting. I went to the fitness center, burned a few hundred calories on the elliptical machine, and drastically reduced my diet. Gone were the McDonald's and the Taco Bell, replaced overnight by low-calorie weight-loss shakes, yogurt, and the occasional turkey sandwich. Of course, it worked . . . for a while. I would lose forty or fifty pounds, and after a few months, I would crash. I even tried running a few times, but instead of taking a systematic approach, I only ran once a week when I got tired of the elliptical machine. I made it through maybe four or five runs before I gave up. Old insecurities would pop up or I'd simply lose motivation. The weight came back every time.

My grandfather was a wealthy restaurateur who left his grandchildren an education trust fund. When I left for college, not only was my tuition and housing already paid for, but I received a twelve-hundred-dollar allowance each month. As lucky as I am to have received a free education, I now realize that this was an unhealthy way for me to go about my schooling. I was never forced to learn the value of a dollar and it was all too easy for me to use that fund to finance my bad habits.

are addictions genetic?

ADDICTION HAS TOUCHED every branch of my family tree—both of my parents, my mom's parents, and her parents' parents have all been affected. (My dad was adopted, so we don't know about his biological parents.) My mom has struggled with her weight throughout her life. Knowing all this, I have never touched a cigarette, illegal drug, or glass of alcohol in my entire life. Yet addiction found its way into my life anyway.

Experts say that there is no such thing as an "addiction gene." However, it may be harder for people with a certain combination of genes to quit certain substances and behaviors once they start. I definitely have an addictive personality. If I enjoy something, I take it to the maximum. This was certainly the case with food, and now it factors into my healthy obsession with running. If you know that addiction runs in your family, do your best to stay away from substances that you might have a hard time quitting. But anyone can find themselves addicted to anything.

If you've become addicted to a substance or behavior that is ruining your life, remember that the same parts of your personality that got you into this mess can get you out. Find a way to focus that addictive obsession on something healthy and positive, and your life will never be the same. My dad's drug addictions came to a head in the 1990s and he was in danger of losing his life. Fortunately, he was able to get it under control and he is now fourteen years sober. Watching my dad hit rock bottom and scratch his way back has shown me that no matter how strong the addiction, no matter how strong the urge, you can always take control.

By then, my weight controlled and influenced every single part of my life. I stayed away from early morning classes because the athletes and other popular kids were in those classes and I didn't want them to see me. I went to restaurants for most meals thanks to my allowance check, but I would go only during off-peak hours so that I wouldn't be around too many people. I remained distant from my family. I didn't want to be seen out and about, so I wouldn't answer phone calls from people who I knew were calling to invite me somewhere. I'd only answer the phone if I already had other plans, so that I already had a built-in excuse.

Somehow, even in the depths of this behavior, I managed to have a girlfriend, Tara, throughout college. One night she suggested that we go to the movies with some of her friends. And why wouldn't she want to go out on a Friday night in college? I, however, wasn't too keen on being social in those days. In fact, going out brought all my doubts and insecurities right to the surface. While Tara or another healthy, fully functioning person might think, *It'll be nice to go out with friends tonight,* my immediate reaction was more like, *What if someone sees me and notices how fat I am? Everyone will judge and ridicule me.* Tara was, of course, sick of staying at home with me, so this time I agreed to go to the movies. At least it would be dark and I could remain hidden—or so I thought.

The five of us got our tickets, bought our movie snacks (a large popcorn and a large Dr Pepper for me, of course), and filed into the theater. By then, I was feeling pretty good. Maybe this night wouldn't be so bad. Maybe I would actually enjoy myself. It *was* nice to be out in the world with other people. The theater was pretty full, but we made our way to a few empty seats. The girls filed in first and I sat down last. I tried to, at least, but I didn't fit. The seat was too small for me. I took a deep breath and tried to force myself in.

Please, God, just let me get in.

But it didn't happen. The handles cut painfully into my hips. But it was much more painful to stand there in a crowded theater, having to tell my girlfriend and her friends that I had to move to the back of the room so that I could take one of the handicapped seats. I tried to hide my embarrassment with lighthearted jokes as usual, but I could feel their pity for me. I tried to hide the tears that night as I lay in bed next to Tara. I tried to hide the fact that I was sneaking to the kitchen to eat more, and more, trying to dull the pain with a few hundred extra calories. Nope, sadness like that isn't something that you just eat away, or smoke away, or gamble away. You know that and I knew that, even then. But I sure did try. It was the only thing I knew how to do.

If there was ever a time to lasso some negative emotion and use it to push myself out of misery, this should have been that moment. I could have used the pain I was feeling as fuel to do something great, something inspired, or something as simple as going for a run. I should have used the anger that I felt toward myself to spark a much-needed change. But I didn't. I had further to fall. Besides, it was easier. Giving up, much like denial, is easy—much easier and more familiar than taking control and starting over.

Days passed. Weeks passed. Months passed.

I would wake up, lie in bed feeling alone and empty, pass some time playing video games, and then try to eat away some misery at the local diner. I ate a fried chicken sandwich, an extra-large order of fries (with a cup of ranch dressing), an order of nachos, a sweet tea, and a peanut butter milkshake for lunch *every day*. Dinner wasn't much

better—usually McDonald's or Taco Bell drive-through while listening to sports radio in the parking lot, feeling much too embarrassed and ashamed to be seen inside.

I was letting myself fall. Eventually, I hit bottom. But it wasn't at the food court or the scale like I would have expected. It was at the blackjack table. Addictions are funny like that. You may have a handle on one of your vices when another one pops up. Addicts refer to this as trading one addiction for another. It makes sense—you need something to fill the void that the previous habit left behind. That's why it's so important to replace your bad habits with something positive and healthy. But I would get to that later. First, I had to fall.

That night, I strolled into the Horseshoe Casino in Tunica, Mississippi, with my friend John to my left and Tara to my right, each of us with our own exaggerated ideas of how successful the night would be. We grabbed some open seats at the Pai Gow table. Our dealer, Hee, remembered us, which I should have taken as a clue that my gambling was a little bit out of control.

Only thirty minutes in, I had burned through two hundred dollars—halfway to my self-imposed "limit." Tara eyed me with concern. I took the easy route (denial) and pretended that I hadn't noticed her gaze as I slid another crisp hundred-dollar bill to Hee.

"Changing one hundred!" he bellowed—a shout of victory for the house. They took my money and gave me some plastic chips, knowing full well that they would get them back soon enough.

Five minutes later, I was down another hundred. When it happens badly, it usually happens quickly. Overeating is often the same way. I looked at Tara. "Let's go to the room," I said. I was deflated, demoralized. Outside, we ran into my friend Guy. He encouraged me to go back to the tables and "get it back."

"I'll be back," I assured him. The addict in me couldn't resist. "I just have to cool down a little. John's at the Pai Gow with Hee. Go get started." We said a temporary good-bye and parted ways. Tara looked at me after they were out of earshot.

"You're going back?" She wasn't happy. Who could blame her? I was already in debt. I was in college with no job. I had no right to be gambling with money I didn't have. But I couldn't stop. I was sad, tired, and desperate.

"It'll be okay," I said. This was an empty promise if there ever was one, and I knew it even as I said the words.

Back in the hotel, neither of us said much, if anything. There was nothing left to say. "I'm going to bed," she said, finally. "Be smart, Ben." She kissed my cheek and went to sleep. I stared at the ceiling a little longer before I grabbed my wallet and headed downstairs.

By midnight, I was down eight hundred fifteen dollars, more than double my limit. That's it, I told myself. I was done. I headed back to the hotel, where at least I could sleep. But as I made my way to the exit, I passed by another ATM, and, like the addict I was—the addict that I am to this day—I chose the easy route yet again, came up with yet another rationalization for my behavior, and took out another hundred eighty-five dollars. I decided to put it all on one hand and if I lost, I would be down an even thousand. The exact numbers didn't matter anymore. They never do. I just needed a good story to tell myself, to justify my fall.

Three seconds later at the blackjack table, I was sitting on sixteen against her king. I waved it off. I couldn't bear to bust and not even have a shot at the money. She turned over a 4. I felt a glimmer of hope. She hit a 5 and took my money before I even had a chance to do the math. It was all over.

I made my way to the sleazy food bar and ate a burger that I had been comped with. If they had asked me to pay for it, I wouldn't have been able to. I made eye contact with the man sitting next to me and immediately recognized myself in his eyes. Neither of us wanted to be there. We were just there because it was the only place we could be. We both had hotel rooms with beds waiting for us, but we hurt too much to sleep. Our expressions told each other the whole story. No one sits alone in a casino eating a burger at three a.m. unless they are at rock bottom.

It was three in the morning. I was down a thousand dollars—a thousand dollars that wasn't even mine. Chase Freedom, what a name. I was, in fact, anything but free. I was trapped—trapped by my own addictions, by my self-hatred, and by my fear. The clangs of the slot machines echoed through to the café. Just hours before, these machines had represented a personal welcome parade of lights and fancy bells, the sounds of victory. But at that moment they just sounded like a death rattle.

Only three hours later, we were making our way home when Tara asked me, "How'd you do?" Her nonchalant inquisition annoyed me. I didn't want to face the truth.

"I didn't do so badly," I replied automatically. "I actually made up a little ground from when you went to bed. I think I lost two or two-fifty."

The sincerity with which I replied—with which I lied—caught even me off guard. I hadn't planned on lying, but I hadn't hesitated, either.

"Oh, not bad. Good job, babe."

She had no reason not to believe me. I was cool on the outside, but inside I was a wreck.

My phone buzzed a little later with a text from a friend wanting to know the same thing as Tara—how did I do?

I replied immediately, again without thinking. "Down about five."

I wasn't just lying to anyone; I was lying to my girlfriend and my best friend. Most of all, I was lying to myself. But that's how these things work. The lies of addiction are a huge part of the cycle that keeps us there. The lies come so easily. They flow because we truly want to believe the things that we're saying. For me, it wasn't just gambling, and it's probably not about just one thing for you, either. I was lying about all of the things that I struggled with on a daily basis, and that was just about every part of my life.

"I haven't actually had much to eat today" translated to "I've eaten a lot more than I should and I really want to eat more." "I got mostly B's. A few C's" actually meant "academic probation and nearly flunking out." "I played about an hour or two of *Mario Kart* earlier. I'm starting to get bored with it" was code for an obsession that consumed me every day.

And here I was, lying about yet another addiction, to the people who knew and loved me most. It was only then that I realized I had hit a new low—financially, physically, and emotionally. My world was spinning right along with the slot machines, and I was completely out of control. I was no longer an inactive, pizza-box-collecting teenager, but the destructive and addictive cycles that had held me back then had only gained traction. I was, by all accounts, an addict, but not necessarily a gambling addict. I was a food addict. Addiction breeds sadness. Sadness breeds bad decisions, often in more than one area. Such are the cycles of an unlived life. I was looking for excitement, for meaning, in all the wrong places.

GOING THROUGH THE MOTIONS

do life

Destructive behavior in one part of life easily leads to other destructive tendencies. I've lived it. But the opposite is true, as well. Once you develop healthy habits that yield positive results, you'll begin to yearn for the healthy, and you'll become addicted just the same. But your new addictions—your addictions to life—will manifest themselves throughout your life in positive ways that you might never have imagined. And while you must still exercise caution so that you don't burn out or go to an extreme in the opposite direction, your new habits will ultimately prove far more exciting than doubling an 11 against a dealer's 6.

Until that night at the casino, it was as if I had been waiting for that elusive moment when I would finally "hit bottom" and turn myself around. In that sense, bottoming out can be a positive thing, because there's only one direction you can go from there. But the truth is that you only bottom out when you decide that *this* is your bottom. If you let yourself, there will always be further to fall. If I hadn't recognized that night at the casino as my bottom, I would have gained more weight, or lost more money, or started some other destructive behavior. So why not make this your bottom? Why not look at the past week or month or year of your life and decide that it's all uphill from here instead of down? Even if your life is great right now, it can always get better.

Remember, thoughts and actions, actions and thoughts. They bounce off each other and spur each other on. When you start thinking positive thoughts, you'll be inspired to take action. If you act positively, you'll begin to think positively. Let's start with this one thought: It's only uphill from here. And, just like that, it's true. No more waiting for change to come to you. It's time to put your thoughts into motion, and the time to start is now.

"Ben, I'm stuck. I know I need to turn my life around, but I have no motivation. Have you ever been stuck? What's your advice?"

The truth is that I was stuck for the first twenty-two years of my life. It's always there; you *know* you need to do something, but you don't. It's overwhelming to even think about. You tell yourself you'll start on Monday, or on the first of next month, or when you buy the right workout DVD.

And when we do start something, a lot of times (especially the first time we try) we go about it the wrong way. I tried so many times to lose weight, but all I knew about weight loss was what I saw in movies or created in my head: *To lose weight, you eat carrots and lettuce, and you become a slave to the treadmill.*

And it's not just about weight loss. We, as humans, look for solutions that will produce quick results. And what breeds quick results? Extreme measures. We set ourselves up for failure before we even begin. We implement unsustainable lifestyles and when they crash and burn (which they almost always do), they crash hard and they burn scars—scars of defeat that serve no purpose but to discourage us from trying again. We get back on the booze, we pick up cigarettes again, and we put the weight back on, plus some.

It's a psychological battlefield and it's not easy to get back on the horse. We are our harshest critics—that's why it's so important to do this the right way. We can't afford to keep failing. So, what is the "right" way? No one knows for sure. But I'm going to try to tell you what I've found in my years of battling. And yes, it's been a

do life

battle. It will always be a battle. I'm okay with that.

So, maybe right now you're here where I was back in 2008. Addicted? Obese? Cut off from the world? Maybe you're not in dire circumstances—maybe you're just looking to improve your life a little. Great. Running won't help just those looking to shift 180 degrees. It can be just a fun way to stay in shape, to lose a few pounds, or keep them off. It can clear your mind or be that little bit of therapy that you need after a long day. Running can bring you closer to your family. It can give you new friends or an excuse to eat cupcakes. It can be whatever you want it to be. Let's get started.

Reader Testimonial

I was 375 pounds and addicted to fast food and video games, playing about sixteen hours or more per day and wasting my life away on Call of Duty. When my grandfather passed away from complications with diabetes after years of deterioration, it was a life-changing shock to my system. With support from my family, I joined a gym and slowly worked off the weight. I fell in love with running and biking and did my first 5K three months after starting out.

Today, I have lost 130 pounds. Not only have I completed more than one marathon, but I am training for my first Ironman Triathlon. I now love my life and although I keep many of my previous Call of Duty skills and am traveling with a pro team, I am also now becoming a firefighter/EMT while in college and triathlon training. I am doing life. —Jason K

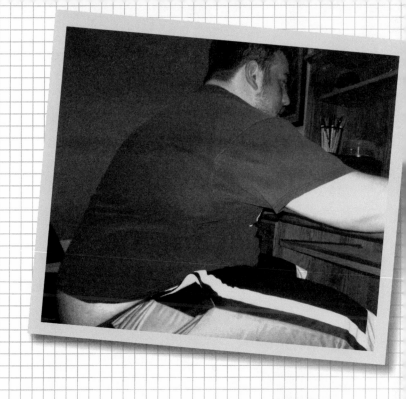

facing the truth

nO MATTER HOW big or small your problems may be, in order to turn things around, you need to decide, once and for all, that the future starts now. To put it simply—you need to take action. My moment came when I started running. If you're looking to make a change, maybe reading this book will be your moment. I truly hope it is.

Without experiencing a moment of clarity, gaining the confidence that tells you that you deserve to finally change your life, and coming up with a specific action to put it into motion, hitting bottom merely represents a new low. Hitting bottom is negative, and change must be positive. You need to channel an inspired, positive thought and turn it into a specific, positive action in order to really make a change.

I admit that I didn't take action immediately after my fateful night at the casino. Instead, I hung out at my new low for a while, feeling as sad as I'd ever been. It felt like I was just waiting, but waiting for what? To die an early death? For someone to come and save me from my own misery?

Luckily, it turns out that I was really just waiting for Meemaw to inspire me to fall in love with running.

My grandma Meemaw called me that November to see if I was planning to come to her house in New England for Christmas with my dad (Pa), as I had done nearly every year as a child. I was despondent in my everyday life, so breaking up the monotony with a winter getaway to New England sounded like a good idea. I told her that I would be there and didn't give it any further thought. Of course, I had no idea at the time that this trip would end up profoundly changing my life. You never know ahead of time which trips, conversations, or adventures will have the greatest impact on your life. That's why you have to show up for all of them, just in case.

My parents had recently divorced. My sister would spend the holidays with my mom, and my brother, Jed, who's five years older than me, was busy with his own life, so it was just Pa and me at Meemaw's house that year. My parents' divorce was remarkably amicable. "We're getting a divorce because we'll be happier when we do," they told us, and that was that. I wasn't close enough to them to be any more involved in the details.

On Christmas Eve, the sun had already set, but the snow on the ground reflected the moonlight so brightly that I could see the backyard clearly through the living room window. Dishes clanged in the kitchen as Pa cleaned up from our lobster dinner. The fire crackled as Meemaw sat working on the crossword puzzle from that morning's paper. I turned to the window and looked into the forest behind her house. I had played in that forest as a child; it's where my brother, Jed, and I had snowball fights and built tree houses. Somewhere in that forest is a time capsule containing little more than crayons and some glue that we buried when we were ten or so years old. I'm sure we'll never dig it back up, but thinking about the time capsule and my childhood made me feel safe and protected.

Meemaw broke the silence, snapping me out of my nostalgia. "What's a three-letter word for 'new-age punk music'?"

I thought for a second. "Does 'ska' fit?"

"Yes. Thanks. I never know the answers to the music questions," she replied.

I shifted the pillow that sat in my lap. Yes, it was a "fat pillow." If you've struggled with your weight for as long as I have, you're probably very familiar with the concept of a fat pillow. The idea is that holding a pillow in your lap will prevent others from seeing exactly how big you really are. I'm pretty sure that keeping a soft, fluffy pillow in your lap actually just makes you look even fatter, but at that point I would have done anything to remain hidden. Facing life, doing life, meant being seen—a truly scary thing for someone who is depressed and morbidly obese. I didn't want anyone to see the real me, how sad and hopeless I really was. I didn't even want to see it myself.

five ways to change your life today

IF YOU'RE HONEST with yourself (and that's the hard part), you can always find something in your life that is holding you back from being the person you want to be. It may take the form of addiction, obesity, an eating disorder, depression, or maybe it's just a rut that you've been stuck in for too long. The important thing is that you identify these and work to fix them. I've made some big progress in righting my ship, and I've done it through running. But I also understand that running, or even fitness of any kind, is not always the answer.

Maybe you're already satisfied with your health. I'm often asked what people should do to change their lives other than the running/triathlon/fitness thing. It's a fair question. To improve the areas of life that you are unsatisfied with, you must replace the bad with something positive that can fill the void. I suggest running, but when that isn't the answer, there are plenty of other things you can do. Here are a few ideas:

1. Join a Volunteer Effort

Become a champion for a cause you believe in by devoting some time every week to volunteering. Giving back is an immensely rewarding experience and will help you feel good about yourself. That good feeling will soon bleed over into all facets of your life.

2. Join a 12-Step Program

If your struggles are based on a dependency that's out of your control, think about joining a program to help get yourself back on your feet. The community and team elements of these programs are enormously helpful and will give you a great start at getting your life back on track.

3. Become Involved in Someone Else's Journey

The people in my life have been crutches for me throughout my journey. It simply wouldn't have been possible without them. Find someone who can use your help and stick with them. Become their biggest fan and be there for them every step of the way. Being invested in someone else's success will motivate you and help you feel great about what you're doing.

4. Go Back to School

It's all about knowledge, baby. Learn a new language, get a new degree, learn to salsa dance, or get certified to be a personal trainer! Look for new and fun ways to further your education and life experience. This new perspective will help you see your life in a whole new way.

5. Take Control of Your Finances

When you live beyond your means or can't stick to a budget, nothing else in your life will feel balanced, either. You'll be surprised by how motivating it is to sit down and figure out a new budget and then work toward sticking to it. This is another example of how healthy living in one area will have a domino effect throughout your life.

Within a few minutes, Meemaw finished the puzzle and set it down on the side table. I'm always amazed by how quickly she finishes the crossword puzzle. She took off her glasses, a sign that she was going to bed. I waited for her to say good night, but instead, she looked at me and smiled. "Merry Christmas, Ben," she said.

"Merry Christmas, Meemaw," I automatically replied.

"Ben?" Meemaw began. I could tell that she wanted to ask me something, and probably not what I wanted for Christmas breakfast, unfortunately. "How are you doing?"

I shifted my eyes nervously. "I'm good. Classes are going well. I'm glad I switched to journalism. I'm enjoying it." I knew that she wasn't really asking me about academics, but I tried to deflect anyway.

"Yeah," she said. "That's good, but what about you? Are you happy?"

I squirmed a little bit. The truth is that I was annoyed, just like I was when Tara had asked me how I had done back at the casino. If you've ever been confronted about your problems before you were a hundred percent ready to make a change, maybe your reaction was similar. It's

do life

uncomfortable to be challenged like this, to be yanked out of denial by someone who knows you and loves you.

Part of the reason that being confronted about your problems is so uncomfortable is that it lets you know exactly how transparent you really are. The fat pillow, the jokes, and all the efforts to remain hidden clearly hadn't worked. It was just like Amanda Gray telling me that I was fat. Everyone already knew. Even worse, they knew before I did. Yet again, someone was telling me what was wrong with me before I was ready to face it. I didn't want to face it. I wanted to take the easy route as always and stay in my comfortable place of denial.

And so I did.

"Yeah, I'm happy," I answered. "Everything is fine. Everything is good." Of course, she knew better, but Meemaw was smart enough to know not to push the issue. She must have known that I had to eventually get there on my own. She could steer me in the right direction, and she always did, but ultimately I would have to choose to face facts and take action myself.

She got up and kissed my forehead. She always kisses my forehead at bedtime.

"Good," she said. "I'm glad. Merry Christmas, sweetheart."

She shuffled upstairs to her bedroom and I sat there, still feeling annoyed. I had no reason to be annoyed, but I was. I didn't want to face this. Why was she making me face this? I went to bed shortly after, but I didn't go to sleep. Meemaw's words echoed over and over in my head. Was I happy? Of course I wasn't. I knew that I wasn't. I had known for a year, at least. It had been, by far, the worst year of my life. I had finally lost Tara, was completely removed from my family, had stopped hanging out with my friends, gambled way too much, and spent the entire year locked in my room playing video games. I knew that I had already hit bottom, but I was still down there, caught in the same destructive cycles that had gotten me to this point.

I started to think about the future, and I immediately began to feel antsy. Living moment by moment like this was one thing, but the idea of living another year like this was terrifying. Contemplating a lifetime like this was impossible. I couldn't do it. Whatever I had to do to prevent a lifetime of this misery would be worth it. Slowly, as I was lying there, an inspiration started to come over me. It was something I hadn't felt in a long time.

I went to the computer and logged in to my blog. I clicked the CREATE A NEW BLOG button. Then I typed the first thing that came into my head: "Ben Does Life." I wasn't sure exactly what it meant, but I would make it mean something. All I knew was that I wasn't doing life at that point. I wasn't living; I was merely surviving, and for the first time I realized that it didn't have to be this way. I had the power to change my life, and it was time to start now.

I crawled back into bed and immediately fell asleep.

The next morning, we opened our Christmas gifts. Meemaw had gotten me a size large shirt from Eddie Bauer. "If it's not the right size, you can exchange it," she said.

"Meemaw, it's three sizes too small," I said, laughing. "But here, look." I handed her a card with the address to the new blog written on it. "I'm getting my life together," I told her. "Don't worry. I bookmarked it for you on the computer. I don't want to return the shirt. . . . I want to fit into it."

I told her about my new plan to get healthy, that I was finally going to lose the weight for good. As we talked, I realized that the difference between the way I felt on that morning and at the beginning of every other failed attempt to lose the weight was that this time it wasn't just about the

FACING THE TRUTH

numbers on the scale or the size of my clothes. Those things were symptoms of the problem, not the real problem itself. I knew that. I finally admitted that. This time, it was about finding the happiness she had asked about. I had spent the better part of two decades as a miserable person, and it was time for a change. It was time to get a grip, to get my life on track. I was going to finally grab life and do life, and I promised her that I would.

"You deserve it," she said. For the first time in a long while, I believed it. That was the first step, and the only real way out of the vicious cycles that had been holding me down. Meemaw had convinced me that I deserved better, and that alone would finally allow me to do better.

After the festivities settled down, I decided to step on Meemaw's scale. This time, I didn't care what the scale said; I just wanted to have a starting point. Every journey has to start somewhere. It doesn't matter where you are today. All that matters is taking the steps to get where you're going. I walked up the steps to her bathroom and stepped on the scale with my eyes closed. The poor thing let out a tortured, high-pitched creak as I unleashed my full weight upon it. I peeked out slowly from behind my hands to survey the damage.

According to the scale, I weighed "ERR."

Of course, I had seen this before. When you spend so many years being obese, you get used to the regular gadgets not working for you: airplane seat belts, blood-pressure cuffs, 360-pound-maximum-weight scales . . . If this had happened a year or even a month before, it would have discouraged me. I would have felt overwhelmed and disgusted with myself, and would immediately have given up on myself before I'd even had a chance to start. But it was truly different this time. Starting at such a low point only motivated me to get started at getting better. It had been a long time since I had felt inspiration like this—probably since *Mario Kart* came out for Nintendo 64.

The truth is that on that morning, I wasn't really sure if this was really it—the one attempt at changing my life that would finally succeed. Maybe this would end up just like every other failed diet I had tried over the years. But finally believing that I deserved to succeed caused me to act differently right from the beginning. While in the past I had always undertaken weight-loss attempts by myself, this time I was inspired to recruit a partner.

This was one of the smartest things I've ever done and a lesson that I can't stress strongly enough. Find a partner. Create a team. Don't allow yourself to remain hidden. If someone's expecting you to show up, you're a million times more likely to show up. When your grandmother is checking your blog for updates, you're five million times more likely to stay on track. When others take notice, they will continue to inspire you. When you get used to the idea of letting yourself down, you won't want to let them down. They will push you and believe in you when you're tempted to give up on yourself. And you'll do the same for them.

That morning was when I first started to understand and appreciate the importance of family. If my family was able to make me feel that I deserved to succeed, maybe they would also help me succeed. If doing life meant going public, then maybe I should reach out. And who would be better to reach out to than someone who's known me my entire life? My brother, Jed, and I were never that close. Being five years apart in age, we always had different friends and different interests, but Jed was overweight himself, weighing in at around 290. Maybe this was something that we could do together. I had no idea how he would react to my random plea to join me in changing my life, but I quickly learned that when you do right, things go right for you. It was as if Jed had been waiting for my call.

"I'm signing us up for a 5K," he said immediately.

And just like that, I came crashing back down to reality. My only running experience up to that point was at the gym during my halfhearted weight-loss attempts. I had never thought that running might be something that would change my life, let alone something I might enjoy. I didn't even know what a 5K was. Was that what those runners were doing when I had to wait for them to pass by the McDonald's driveway on some Saturday mornings? The term *race*, more than anything else, freaked me out. Races are for fast people, I thought. Races are for runners, and there was simply no way that I was a runner. I felt myself slipping backward into the old thinking about who I was and who I wasn't.

misconceptions about runners and running

BEFORE I STARTED running, I believed that runners were just plain different from me. They were crazy gluttons for punishment. They were all crunchy, granola health nuts. They never struggled with their weight or self-image or the constant temptation to hit the snooze button and skip a run. Of course, I was wrong. Here are a few more of the most common myths about runners and running that I hear, and the truth behind them.

1. If you run a marathon, you're going to die of a heart attack

When I talk to nonrunners about the running I do, a frequent response I get is "I would run a marathon, but I'm too scared of having a heart attack like you see on the news all the time." The truth is that the reason you see those heart attacks on the news is that they're so rare. If they happened at every race, they wouldn't be newsworthy. It's like airplanes—the crashes make the news because they're sensationalistic and atypical. You never see a headline about the millions of flights that go off without a hitch. *The New England Journal of Medicine* published a report in January of 2012 stating that in a ten-year study of eleven million runners, only fifty-nine of them suffered heart attacks during races. If you're still concerned, get approval from your doctor before beginning your training. (This is a good idea for all beginning runners, too.)

2. You have to spend a lot of time stretching before a run to avoid injuries

Before a race, it's pretty common to see people bending over to touch their toes or sitting on the ground with their legs split, dramatically stretching their muscles to the limit in an effort to "loosen" them up. However, most experts these days encourage a few minutes of light jogging to warm up and post-run stretching to avoid injuries. I've found this to be true, and I never stretch before running. I simply jog in place for a few minutes, and I always feel better as a result. Postrace stretches always feel great.

3. Strength training isn't important for runners

To put it simply—yes, it is. You will become a much stronger runner if you devote a few hours a week to strength training in addition to your running regimen. Runners use their core, shoulders, and arms a lot more than you might think. If you put the time in on the weights, you will not only be far less prone to injury, but you'll be pleasantly surprised by how much your running performance improves.

4. Running is bad for your joints

I often hear running naysayers make sarcastic comments like "Have fun with your hip and knee replacements after doing all that running." Conventional wisdom does say that running will damage your joints, but in this case conventional wisdom is wrong. Recent studies show that there is actually no connection between running and arthritis. Even better, running may actually prevent joint problems from arising.

5. Training for races will leave you with no time for a social life

This one is simply based on bad math. Even at peak marathon training, a runner will be facing anywhere from thirty to forty miles per week, which comes down to an average of forty-five minutes to an hour of running a day. If you can't find that much time in your day to run, a social life should be the least of your worries.

Even though Jed was also overweight, the adventure races that he'd done with my dad had given him a more realistic perspective on what we needed to do. "Look," he said, "we don't have to run the whole thing. And we're sure as hell not going to be worried about winning. But we have this motivation now; we have to make sure to put it into action. We have to have something to work toward."

He couldn't have been more right. Thoughts are an essential part of the cycles that will push you toward healthy or unhealthy behavior, but they are nothing without the behaviors themselves. You can spend all day thinking great things about yourself, but if you don't change your routines and habits, those thoughts will get you nowhere. We had to jump in. A 5K it was—whatever that was. We were scared, but we were ready. And we were already on our way.

"Ben, what's your biggest piece of advice?"

Share the journey. It is crucial to have a strong support system in place before making a big life change. There were so many times that I didn't want to work out but was saved by having different accountability systems in place. I've separated my groups into friends, family, an online community, a fitness center community, and running clubs. They all provide something different. Friends and family will be there to talk to you about the more personal or emotional sides of the whole journey. They'll also keep tabs on you by checking in and asking how everything is going. It helps when the people you spend the majority of your time with are invested in your progress right along with you.

Joining a gym or a weekly fitness class will also increase the likelihood of your success. For more than half a year in the beginning, I forged friendships through our local boot camp class that really kept me motivated to sticking with the plan, both fitness- and dietwise. If you just sneak into the gym to do the treadmill for thirty minutes a day, you might feel inspired the first few weeks, but that superficial feeling will fade. Surrounding yourself with people, holding conversations, a collective group mentality . . . these are the things that are going to keep you coming back. Join something. Pay money to join something. It's imperative that you feel part of something bigger than just watching a thirty-minute exercise DVD. It's not about exercise; it's about healthy and fun living.

Join an online support group. Some of my best friends are people I've met through Web sites and blogs while sharing our weight-loss stories. There's no excuse

not to join different forums, message boards, and exercise social networks. There are specific mediums for just about every type of journey. Put yourself out there. You get what you give. Online, you'll find yourself connecting with people and sharing successes and setbacks together in a convenient format. I also suggest blogging and the health and fitness communities in the blogosphere. I know blogging is not for everyone. It's just that I know how strong and helpful the communities are, so I preach that gospel.

Running clubs are priceless. Do a simple Google search to find running clubs in your town. You're so much more likely to stick with the program if you're committed to specific individuals to show up on a regular basis and do group runs or races. These people are going to become your friends and will make the weekly long run seem like a breeze. Soon, they'll become social events that you will actually look forward to. And isn't that the whole point? Work to make your fitness regime feel less like work, and you'll get more out of it than you may ever have imagined.

Reader Testimonial

I was always a big kid. I was teased, picked on, ridiculed—the usual punishment for someone who eats too many E.L. Fudge cookies and Reese's Peanut Butter Cups. A big part of my growing up years consisted in death (father when I was three, grandparents at ten, another grandpa at sixteen), and in my adolescence, all I knew was pain and heartbreak. I was diagnosed with depression, anxiety, and panic attacks, and labeled as suicidal. I weighed 275 pounds. I was miserable.

Aided by clashes in medication, my life spiraled out of control. I'll spare the details for now, but I ended up hospitalized. There, in the midst of my darkest days of my life, I decided that I was going to overcome these obstacles. When I was released, I was a new person—driven and inspired to change. I lifted weights. I played football. I ran. I busted my butt on the elliptical. I rebuilt relationships with my family and friends. I graduated from high school at 197 pounds. I will never forget when my mom looked at me with tears in her eyes and said, "I got my son back."

After that, I became content. I went to college. I started getting back into my old eating habits. I moved. I went to grad school. I kept eating. During grad school, I found myself at the heaviest I ever was—284 pounds. I literally had conversations with a friend about wondering if I was addicted to food. The scary part was genuinely not knowing the answer. So I went for a run. Half a mile at first. Then slowly (really slowly), I progressed. I ran my first 5K and instantly became addicted. I kept going. I moved again this past July, and since then I have truly developed a love (and sometimes hate) for running. Over the past year and a half, I have completed nineteen races (all 5K to 10K). I have dropped sixty-plus pounds, and am approaching my newfound goal of losing seventy-five-plus for the second time in my life.

A week from Sunday, I will be running my first half marathon, and I am about one crazy impulse away from signing up for my first marathon in October. I have found my happiness again, and a confidence that I have never had in my life. But best of all, I have had a lot of people in my life come up and tell me that I inspire them. I have had so many people help me through my journey, but I never would have expected to have had that same impact on anyone else. To me, that is the greatest gift. —Alan P

FACING THE TRUTH

hitting the pavement

YOU MAY HAVE a moment like I did with Meemaw, when you feel that inspiration come over you and you fill up with hope and encouragement. And the difference between success and failure lies in Jed's simple words: You have to put those feelings into action. Thoughts and actions, right? When you have the right thoughts, you need to immediately put them into action. If you waste a moment or wait a day, a negative thought might come along and tempt you to put that into action, instead.

My dad has successfully kicked a nasty drug habit that plagued him for decades, and he credits the following quote from a counselor with helping him finally do it: "You have to act your way into right thinking." He once told me that when he first heard this, it struck him as funny and backward. He had always fancied himself a thinking man, and he assumed that once he got his mind right, he'd be able to do whatever was necessary to get where he needed to be. The trouble, of course, was that while he was using drugs, his mind was terribly skewed, and totally incapable of healthy, rational thought. It was only after he took healthy action that his thinking came around.

The same thing is true for kicking any habit, or simply living the life you want to live. When you're in a bad place, the negative thoughts spur the negative actions, and vice versa. You tell yourself, "You're a fat slob," and then you eat an entire pizza, or you eat an entire pizza and then you tell yourself, "You're a fat slob." It doesn't matter which way it goes, but in order to turn it around, you have to change one or both of them. I know from experience that it's a lot easier to change your actions than it is to change your entire way of thinking.

So instead of the pizza, you force yourself to eat a healthy meal, and instead of playing video games, you force yourself to run around the track. You act your way out of your rut, and eventually your thoughts will follow you in the right direction. At some point, you'll find yourself thinking about yourself and your life in an entirely different way. Your actions will make you feel good, and good thoughts, positive energy, and true change will follow.

Before having that conversation with Jed, I had only run a couple of times in my life, but at that moment, all I wanted to do was run. I couldn't wait to strap on some sneakers and hit the pavement. It was something I wanted to do, something that I finally realized I needed to do.

"Okay," I told Jed. "I'm in." We signed up for a 5K that was being held only seventeen days later. Sometimes in life, you just have to jump in. Commit yourself before you can question it and find an excuse to back out. If you hesitate for a moment, there will always be a reason to wait longer, and then to never get back around to doing it. When will you ever feel completely ready? When will you ever have all the perfect equipment, the exact right frame of mind, the free time, the money, and any other thing you can possibly tell yourself that you need before you can finally get going? I'll tell you when—never. If you wait for everything to align before making a change, you'll be waiting forever.

You can start a journey a million different ways—with a carefully mapped-out plan, a rough guide, or with only your instincts to guide you. My new life was set to start immediately, but I had no idea where to begin. Jed and I had no official training guide, no *Runner's World* subscriptions, and no real grasp on how to get cracking, so we just did what felt natural, and we felt our way through the process.

a word on treadmills

OVER THE PAST four years, I've run over three thousand miles in nearly every condition you can imagine. I've run through downpours, tornado warnings, blizzards, 120-plus degree scorchers—you name it. Not one of those miles, however, has been run on a treadmill, and that is for a very simple reason. I have a personal vendetta against treadmills, and it's as a result of this grudge that I have become a purist, only doing my runs outdoors or on indoor tracks.

One of my first attempts at running was on a treadmill. Shortly after signing up for our first 5K, Jed and I walked into the fitness center, ready to embark on our newfound voyage. We strutted up to the treadmill and cranked it on. Jed began jogging without any trouble, but once my machine got going and I started to jog, the impact of my weight on the landings was too much for the mechanism. The belt stopped abruptly, nearly tripping me. It was horribly embarrassing and actually quite scary, and I still haven't forgiven that particular brand of treadmills. It seems to me that a treadmill company would spend some extra money to make sure that this type of thing didn't happen to the exact consumer they are trying to target.

Of course, you needn't allow my personal resentments to prevent you from putting in some miles on a treadmill. Many of my running friends have done so, and Pa once knocked out an eighteen-miler on the belt. One thing you should know beforehand is that running on a treadmill is physically easier than running outdoors. One reason is that there is no wind resistance on a treadmill. If you run outside on a calm day, you will be facing wind at the speed at which you're running. If you're running a ten-minute mile, the wind is pushing you at six miles per hour. If you're running into a headwind, it gets even harder. You would need a tailwind at least equal to your running speed in order to emulate treadmill running. The other main difference with running on the ground is that you have to use more muscles to propel yourself forward. Treadmills do a lot of the "forward" movement for you, allowing your muscles more rest.

These differences are relatively minor. Don't feel like you're slacking if you prefer to run on a treadmill; just make sure that you are pushing yourself during your workouts. Running on a treadmill is certainly a lot better than not running at all. The worst thing about treadmill runs is that they're incredibly boring. My best advice is to find the ones with built-in TV screens and start your run at the beginning of an episode of *CSI*.

Jed and I quickly learned not to expect too much of ourselves too soon. Don't get greedy. Journeys don't start and finish overnight. Allow yourself to have fun in the process. The first few months of a running journey are when you're going to learn the nuances of the sport, when you're going to see and feel the most dramatic changes to your body. Enjoy these moments and celebrate each small accomplishment without expecting too much of yourself. Allow yourself to crawl before you walk, and then to feel each step as you go.

The same thing goes for kicking any bad habit. Celebrate the small successes. AA and other similar programs give out chips to symbolize milestones along the way to sobriety, and this is a good model for anyone who is trying to make a change for the better. Reward yourself for a good day, a good week, and then for a good month or year. Tell your loved ones how many days it has been since your last pizza or cigarette or pill. Allow them to celebrate with you, and to continue to cheer you on.

I didn't know the "right" way to run, so I literally went out to the street and ran to the first stop sign. Then I walked a little. Then I ran to the next one. Experts would call this "interval training," but you don't need experts or lingo in order to do it. Go out each day and eyeball a stop sign, mailbox, or power line seventy-five or so yards away. Run to it. Walk until you've caught your breath, and then seek out another one and run some more.

With my 365 pounds, running was a constant battle. Each step jarred my skeleton as the earth's gravity pulled my mass back down to the solid ground. My stomach and man boobs bounced painfully as I pushed myself beyond my very restricted physical limits. At first, I managed to run for only eight minutes. I say "run," but it was more like a shuffle, a molasses-like trot. As humbling as it was at the time, I now look back on those days with nostalgia and think, *I remember when I gave everything I had and it only added up to eight torturous minutes.* I'm proud of my former self for hanging in there when it was so tough.

So start by running to the stop sign, and then try running past the stop sign. I ran my first mile without stopping just a couple of days after we started running, and before I knew it, we were heading out for our first 5K. I weighed 350 pounds, had only been jogging for two weeks, and had no

HITTING THE PAVEMENT

idea what to expect. When we arrived, I sat in the truck with Jed and watched a crowd of runners going through their stretching routines. They were real runners. And what was I? I looked at them in awe, thinking that they were different from me—a different species entirely. I didn't realize then that the only difference between being a runner and not being a runner is simply the act of running.

do life runner's commandments

Thou Shalt Not Do Too Much Too Soon

You will find this one highlighted in every running advice article worth its salt, and for good reason. You will go down in flames if you do not heed it. Marathons aren't trained for overnight. Pace yourself.

Thou Shalt Run in the Morning

Too much can happen if you put your run off until night. You're tired from work; you have to cook dinner for your kids; *American Idol* is on. . . . Nothing else is happening at five thirty a.m., though. Get out there and get it done before the rest of the world even wakes up. You'll thank yourself at six thirty p.m. when you're kicked back in your recliner. Trust me. Yes, it sucks to wake up, but only for the first week or two. You'll get used to it.

Thou May Run with an iPod, but Thou Shalt Not Become a Slave to It

This is a controversial one. The vast majority of runners these days have buds in their ears blaring the latest Black Eyed Peas single, and there's nothing wrong with that. (Well, you know, other than the Black Eyed Peas part.) But you'll be surprised by how pleasant running

can be without music to distract you. Enjoy the wind
whistling, waves crashing, Honda Civics backfiring . . .

Thou Shalt Run in the Rain and Snow

First of all, you'll look like a certified badass to everyone
passing you in a car. Plus, it's not as bad as it looks.
Technological advances have made it remarkably easy
to feel comfortable even in the toughest conditions.
There are spikes for running in ice, insulated rain jackets
for keeping dry in the most severe of monsoons, and
sexy tights for keeping warm even in CANADA!

Thou Shalt Not Compare Thyself to Other Runners

We don't run to win; we run to become better. We run to
keep our sanity. We run to find out what we're capable
of. There is no mandatory speed that you need to hit
in order to be known as a "runner." If you run, you're a
runner. Don't look at what other people are doing; you'll
just drive yourself crazy.

Thou Shalt, However, Compete Maniacally with Yourself

The two most important letters in running are PR—
Personal Record. You might be content with jogging a
couple of times a week to clear your mind or whatever,
but taking it up a level to the racing scene, the PR scene,
will only make running more fun. You'll learn to yearn for
those increasingly elusive PRs and work to get better
because of them.

Thou Shalt Check Yourself Out in Store Windows, but Thou Shalt Be Careful

You have to make sure that no one sees you, because
they will know what you're doing and you will look like

a buffoon. Also, watch out for telephone poles (not that I would know from experience or anything).

Thou Shalt Occasionally Turn Off the GPS Device

GPS devices are magical little gadgets that measure our every step and map our routes through our lovely cities. Kick it old-school every so often, though. It will prove to be a liberating experience. There will be no fretting over lost seconds at intersections, new routes to never-before-seen areas, and no waiting around locating satellites.

Thou Shalt Listen to Thy Body

It's always better to miss a few days while resting a nagging pain than to power through and end up missing three months because the nagging ache turns into a full-blown injury. It's easy to get stubborn and think that you have to be "macho" and gut it out, but you'll almost always end up with a running ban from your doctor and an agonizing sense of regret. Rest is one of the most important aspects of any training regimen.

Thou Shalt Use Lube Liberally

This is one I wish I had known at the beginning of my running career. Armpits, inner thighs, nipples, feet—BODYGLIDE is your friend. Take my word for it, or you're in for some agonizing post-run showers.

Thou Shalt Wear Reflective Gear and Even Then Stay Vigilant

Assume that every driver out there is your nearly blind eighty-eight-year-old grandmother. Run against traffic. Keep an eye open for swervy drivers and err on the side of caution when they are passing at high speeds—cheat inland a few steps.

Thou Shalt Not Be Afraid to Carb-Load

This is one of the greatest pleasures of running. Typically, these guilt-free pasta-fests are advised two to three days before a race and only for distances of half marathon or higher. For a 5K, you can get away with a mild one-meal carb load, more for the novelty's sake than actual race performance.

My friend John joined me and Jed for the 5K in a much-appreciated show of support. Seeing the tortured look on my face as we lined up, he quickly assured me that he'd run every step of the way with me. I couldn't back out now. John was here with me and I was accountable. If you don't have a friend like John or a partner like Jed who will run with you, sign up for a 5K today anyway. You'll meet other runners at your level that you can plan to hang out with at future races. Surrounding yourself with like-minded individuals who will hold you accountable is a huge catalyst for a life in running, and what better place to forge these friendships than at a race?

The gun went off, and so did we. After five minutes, I was near the back of the pack, which was fine with me. If you're nervous about signing up for your first race, start out with a 5K, and don't worry—there will always be someone who finishes behind you. Virtually all races these days have a walking division, ensuring that your fear of finishing last is not a valid excuse to stay away. For me, this wasn't about winning. My running will never be about winning. It's about doing something, doing life, and doing it the best I can.

Plod, plod, plod. Huff, puff, huff.

I was twenty minutes in and the winners had already been done for three minutes. My joints were aching and my feet were numb, but I was overcome with a resolve to finish the

race strong. A nice old man pointed out the halfway mark to me, and as tough as it was, as heavy as I felt, I knew that each remaining step I took meant that I was closer to the end rather than the beginning, like a golf ball as it passes the peak of its arc. Now I just needed to fall back to earth, slow and steady.

There was less than a mile to go. Ahead of me, I saw Jed finish. I had to push myself to go on. I told myself that one day I would beat him in a race, but this was not the day. As I reached the top of the hill that led down toward the finish line, I suddenly felt a burst of confidence. I was really going to finish this thing. I pushed harder, sprinted the final forty meters, and smiled for the finish-line camera, crossing the line with my hands in the air. In my head, I was starring in my own movie. I heard the fireworks and the swell of the music in my head, and I knew for the first time that I was really on my way. I was changing my life. Now all I had to do was keep going.

"What's next?" Jed asked, as we celebrated over breakfast after the race. And, once again, he was right. Today was only the beginning of my journey. I was nowhere near the end. But I knew that I was on the right track, because for once I couldn't wait to see what was next.

▶ **READER QUESTION**

"Ben, I struggle with self-esteem, self-confidence, and self-doubt. What advice do you have for me?"

You're not the only one.

I've spent the majority of my life dealing with a bad self-image. When I started running, I was ashamed of how I looked and feared that people would mock me. At that first 5K with Jed, I felt like I didn't belong there with the other runners, even though I completed the race just like they did. This is something I still battle today. But last year, just after I boarded flight 4692, service from Salt Lake City to Oklahoma City, I had a breakthrough.

"Ma'am?" The pleasant man in the seat next to mine was trying to get the flight attendant's attention. She scurried down the aisle and greeted him. "Is that seat vacant?" He motioned in the direction of the seat in question. She told him she'd check and scurried off.

I'll be honest; I was a little crushed. I was pretty sure I didn't smell bad, and I don't take up too much room. In fact, I was a good inch and a half from the armrest. By all accounts, we had a pleasurable conversation. (His name was Phil, and he was an engineer based out of Oklahoma. He was headed home after a business trip.) I didn't overgreet. I tend to err on the side of less is more when it comes to flying conversations.

I glanced back to check out the seat he was asking about. It was an aisle seat—just like his. It was next to another passenger—just like his. Granted, the passenger was a lady (and mildly attractive), but still . . . The flight attendant returned and confirmed that the seat was, in fact, available. Phil grabbed his Starbucks drink and gathered his belongings to head back to his new chair.

My instinct was to stop him, sit him down, and request an exit interview. I wanted to figure out what I could have done better to keep him as a flight partner. Our natural instinct is to want explanations. But before I could, as if he knew the insecurities racking my brain, he looked back and erased my fears.

"No offense, bud. I just want to sit next to my cousin. We couldn't book our seats together." Well, that was a simple and reasonable explanation. I felt so much

better. But the whole situation brought about a startling realization. My first reaction was to think, *What's wrong with me? What did I do wrong?* Being the curious type—I'm always trying to figure out why things occur—I began some introspective thinking.

Where does this insecurity come from? It's not hard to nail that down. I grew up in a very self-conscious shell. Being overweight my whole life certainly had negative impacts of my self-worth and self-image. I was constantly overcompensating with outrageous behavior—both inward outrageous (fifteen to twenty hours a day in front of a screen playing computer games) and outward (making *Jackass*-style videos and that whole "green-hair phase").

Now I look in the mirror and I see a relatively normal-looking guy—a somewhat educated, somewhat intelligent (despite my father's claims to the contrary) young man. Sure, there's the infamous duct tape incident (which I'm still not comfortable sharing) and the whole pizza box fiasco . . . But still, I feel better than I ever have. I look as good as I ever have. I'm happier than I've ever been.

Why, then, do I still assume there's something wrong with me when issues arise? And it's not just me. I've realized this is a common theme. Most people assume the worst. We beat ourselves up and we blame ourselves even when it's not rational or logical. We pathologically worry what people are thinking of us, so much so that we begin to think poorly of ourselves.

It seems to me that we're wasting a lot of time beating ourselves into the ground. Yeah, we've lost weight or run marathons or fit into that goal bikini; we've come a long way, but our mind still has a lot of work to do. Let's start by not assuming we're to blame, because, more often than not, we're actually not. I almost let the fear of running in public stop me from starting this journey to begin with, but the truth is that nobody was pointing and laughing at me when I joined that 5K as I feared. They were too busy focusing on their own races. So when that guy leaves you sitting alone in seat 21E, remind yourself, he's missing out. And smile, sit back, relax, and enjoy the flight.

Reader Testimonial

Slow and steady wins the race.

We are the Turtles—a group of women of different ages, backgrounds, and locations. We have two things in common: Weight Watchers and Couch to 5K. We met on the Weight Watchers message boards in the first half of 2011. Specifically, we all posted in the daily Couch to 5K thread. Throughout the C25K program, we encouraged each other and supported each other, and together we learned what it meant to be runners.

We each have our own obstacles to overcome to pursue an active and healthy lifestyle: some of us are married, have kids, and work full-time, others are stay-at-home moms caring for multiple kids, still others are living the single life and trying to balance an active social life with healthy habits. We are in our thirties, forties, and fifties. We live in Florida, California, Wisconsin, Texas, and everywhere in between. Some of us have been "chunky" our whole lives, and others gained weight after pregnancy or a significant life event. Some of us were athletes in high school; others had never really voluntarily exercised.

Since early 2011, we have lost over five hundred pounds

HITTING THE PAVEMENT

as a group. Some of us have achieved "Lifetime" status with Weight Watchers. These individuals have met their weight goal and have maintained it for weeks and months. Some of us are still losing, whether we have ten pounds to go or another thirty pounds or even sixty pounds still to go.

After the initial 5K races at the conclusion of the Couch to 5K program, many of us began dreaming big. We have run numerous 5Ks, some 10Ks, and a handful of us have run half-marathons. One Turtle is currently training for a full marathon in the fall. Some other turtles have started considering or training for duathlons and triathlons.

In March of 2011, we had our first official Turtle Trek. Many of us met in Virginia Beach, Virginia, for the Townebank Shamrock 8K over St. Patrick's Day. And a handful of our Midwest Turtles met for a 7K in Minnesota. It was the first time most of us had met in person, and we spent a weekend bonding and trying on our "fat pants."

A dozen of us Turtles are now registered to run the Ragnar Relay from Miami to Key West in January 2013.

When we were all still plugging our way through the Couch to 5K program, we lamented about how slowly we all ran: thirteen-, fourteen-, fifteen-minute miles. Yet we were a tough group—determined and unwilling to give up. Hence, we named ourselves the Turtles (shortened from the original "Weight Watchers Couch to 5K or WW C25K Turtles"). We may have been slow, but we were doing it!　　　　　　　　　　　　　—Jennifer C

5K TRAINING GUIDE

Five kilometers, or 3.1 miles, is by far the most popular race distance in the world today. It is constructed to be long enough to warrant training, but short enough to be doable for people all across the board. The fastest runners will finish the 5K in fewer than fifteen minutes. The majority of us, though, are somewhere between twenty minutes and sixty minutes. Don't take the distance lightly if you are just starting out; it does take time to work up to.

I'm constructing this guide along with my personal trainer, Suzanne. I'm basing it on my experiences through running and Suzanne's credentials and knowledge of the body. It is a ten-week guide geared to beginners aiming to run their first 5K.

WEEK ONE

DAY ONE: walk 15–20 minutes

DAY TWO: rest

DAY THREE: alternate 30 seconds jogging/2 minutes walking for 20 minutes

DAY FOUR: alternate 1 minute jogging/90 seconds walking for 25 minutes

DAY FIVE: rest

DAY SIX: alternate 1 minute jogging/1 minute walking for 25 minutes

DAY SEVEN: walk 15 minutes

WEEK TWO

DAY ONE: alternate 1 minute jogging/1 minute walking for 30 minutes

DAY TWO: rest

DAY THREE: alternate 3 minutes jogging/2 minutes walking for 30 minutes

DAY FOUR: walk 5 minutes, jog 13 minutes, walk 15 minutes

DAY FIVE: rest

DAY SIX: jog 15 minutes

DAY SEVEN: walk 20 minutes

WEEK THREE

DAY ONE: run 1 mile

DAY TWO: cross-train, stretch

DAY THREE: run 1 mile, walk 15 minutes

DAY FOUR: run 1.25 miles

DAY FIVE: rest

DAY SIX: run 1.5 miles, walk 15 minutes

DAY SEVEN: walk 30 minutes

WEEK FOUR

DAY ONE: run 2 miles

DAY TWO: rest, stretch

DAY THREE: run 1.5 miles

DAY FOUR: run 1.25 miles

DAY FIVE: rest

DAY SIX: run 2 miles

DAY SEVEN: jog 2 miles

WEEK FIVE

DAY ONE: run 2 miles

DAY TWO: rest, stretch

DAY THREE: run 2.25 miles

DAY FOUR: run 2 miles

DAY FIVE: rest

DAY SIX: run 2.5 miles

DAY SEVEN: jog 2 miles

WEEK SIX

DAY ONE: run 2.25 miles

DAY TWO: rest, stretch

DAY THREE: run 2 miles

DAY FOUR: run 2.25 miles

DAY FIVE: rest

DAY SIX: run 2.5 miles

DAY SEVEN: jog 2 miles

5K training guide

WEEK SEVEN

DAY ONE: run 2.25 miles

DAY TWO: rest, stretch

DAY THREE: run 2.5 miles

DAY FOUR: run 2.5 miles

DAY FIVE: rest

DAY SIX: run 2.75 miles

DAY SEVEN: jog 2 miles

WEEK EIGHT

DAY ONE: run 2.5 miles

DAY TWO: rest, stretch

DAY THREE: run 2.25 miles

DAY FOUR: run 1 mile, timing yourself. Go fast.

DAY FIVE: rest

DAY SIX: run 2.75 miles

DAY SEVEN: jog 1.5 miles

WEEK NINE

DAY ONE: run 2.5 miles

DAY TWO: rest, stretch

DAY THREE: run 3 miles

DAY FOUR: run 2 miles

DAY FIVE: rest

DAY SIX: run 3 miles

DAY SEVEN: jog 2 miles

WEEK TEN

DAY ONE: rest

DAY TWO: run 3 miles

DAY THREE: rest

DAY FOUR: walk 30 minutes

DAY FIVE: rest

DAY SIX: rest

DAY SEVEN: RACE DAY

When you finish your first 5K, don't spend too much time worrying about your finish time. Finishing strong and running your race should be the only two goals for your first. You're going to improve and you're going to get a lot faster.

Here's how I progressed from my first 5K to my fastest 5K:

First 5K: 40 minutes 13 seconds
Second 5K: 32 minutes 38 seconds
Third 5K: 31 minutes 18 seconds
Fourth 5K: 29 minutes 7 seconds
Fifth 5K: 27 minutes 58 seconds
Eighth 5K: 25 minutes 48 seconds

Tenth 5K: 23 minutes 25 seconds
Twelfth 5K: 22 minutes 1 second

I shaved eighteen minutes off the 5K distance in just over a year. Get excited; watching yourself get faster is one of the coolest things about starting running, and 5K is the perfect distance to gauge yourself.

fun 5k facts

- Men's World Record: 12 minutes 37 seconds (4:03 minutes per mile)

- Women's World Record: 14 minutes 11 seconds (4:33 minutes per mile)

- The 5K has been raced in the Olympics since the Olympic Games in Stockholm in 1912 for men and since the Atlanta Olympics in 1996 for women.

pacing yourself

a S IMPORTANT AS it is to dive headfirst into your new life instead of plotting and planning and procrastinating for as long as possible, it's equally essential to set goals and find a comfortable rhythm for your progress. Think about it this way—the people who are just going, going, going without pausing to think about what they're doing or why they're doing it are usually headed in the wrong direction. When I was depressed and addicted, I didn't set goals for my weight gain or my lethargy, and if your life is off-kilter, you probably didn't plan for that, either.

But it's not enough to simply set goals. You have to set the *right* goals, in the right order, at the right time. Look at New Year's resolutions, for example. They are almost always cast aside by the time Valentine's Day rolls around, and that's for two very simple reasons—a majority of those resolutions or goals are too big and too vague. How many times have you (or one of your friends) said, "This is the year I'll get healthy" or "I'm going to quick smoking this year"? And when New Year's Day came, you threw out all your cigarettes or maybe you found yourself at the gym, signing up for a membership with all the other January suckers. Most gyms even offer discount memberships throughout the month of January because they know that the vast majority of members who join right after the New Year will be gone before long.

Sure enough, after a few weeks go by and you start to feel stressed or antsy, you tell yourself, "I'm doing pretty good; I can ease up on myself a little," and you buy a pack of cigarettes or skip the gym for a few days, and before long your old habits are right back where they used to be. So, why does this happen? It's because without specific, quantifiable goals, you don't know how to measure your success or failure. You work out for three weeks straight, but you don't know whether that means you've reached your goal or are on the way to meeting your goal. You can't leave room for any doubt, or you'll go back to your old vices and comfortable patterns every time.

If your goal is to start running, your ultimate goal really shouldn't be "I'm going to start running." It should be something more along the lines of "I'm going to run a 5K by March and a 10K by this summer" or "I'm going to run a mile five days a week." With goals like these, you can check in with yourself and know exactly how you're doing and where you are in your process. You only ran three days so far this week? Okay, then run two more. It's February and you're nowhere near being able to run a 5K? Okay, start training more right now. For a runner or simply for someone with a goal, numbers are your best friend, because they are quantifiable and measurable. Always include specific numbers in your goals.

The other reason that those New Year's resolution–types of goals don't work is that they're too big and overwhelming. When I was faced with the state of my health in fifth grade, tenth grade, and then again in college, I couldn't get myself to make a change because the task at hand was enormous, immeasurable. I literally didn't know where to start.

Likewise, if I had left Meemaw's house after experiencing my lightbulb moment with her and said, "I'm going to run a marathon this year," I never would have succeeded. I would have doubted myself and become overwhelmed and given up immediately. Coming up with a more reasonable goal, to run a 5K in seventeen days (as unreasonable as it seemed at the time), set me up for success in ways I never could have imagined. Small goals like running a 5K and then a 10K can, of course, lead to larger goals like running a marathon or completing an Ironman. In fact, lining up your goals like this will make those ultimate goals so much more realistic, because they are now broken down into smaller, far more obtainable chunks.

In life, you never get to go from A to Z in one jump. You dive in, go from A to B, and then you can go on to C. You hop to D and E and F. Before long, you'll end up at Z, but you'll do so in a realistic and healthy way. It's like driving a car in a dense fog. You can't see what's at the end of the road; you can only see what's next, what's right in front of you, and what (in that moment) is most important. That's how goals have to be.

Of course, this doesn't just apply to running, or losing weight, or even battling addiction. This goes for every goal in life. You want to get married and have kids before turning forty? Okay, start by breaking it down into smaller, specific goals: Get on an online dating site, commit to e-mailing at least three interesting-looking people a week. Or do you want to get a new job in a different field? The same techniques should apply to you. Start by taking courses in your new field, updating your résumé, and applying to at least one job every day.

do life

YOU HAVE TO think of your goals in as specific terms as possible in order to ensure success. Here are a few examples of goals that are too vague and how you can change them to be more explicit:

> If your goal is "I want to get stronger," change this to "I will work to do fifty push-ups without stopping in eight weeks."

> If your goal is "I want to lose weight," change this to "I will lose eight pounds in four weeks."

> If your goal is "I want to start running," change this to "I will run a half marathon by my thirtieth birthday."

> If your goal is "I want to eat healthier," change this to "I will maintain a diet journal and stick with my eating plan."

> If your goal is "I want to get faster," change this to "I will shave five minutes off my 10K PR."

Jed and I were now a team, and we committed to doing these races together. For us, setting goals revolved around signing up for one race, and then another, and another. We did them all together so that we remained accountable and kept each other on track. We signed up for another 5K and finished that one. Then we signed up for another and did another one. We signed up for boot camp classes together to keep us motivated and moving forward. I was running daily and getting faster. I was losing weight and feeling happier. My brother and I were sharing a closer relationship than we'd ever had, even when we were kids. My perspective was slowly changing from a depressed, negative outlook to a more positive one. Like my dad taught me, I was acting my way into thinking right.

But I was still overweight, and I wasn't yet what I would describe as "healthy." So why was I suddenly finding the smile that had eluded me for so many years? It's because just by starting and reaching my first small goal, I was starting a new cycle of positive actions leading to happy thoughts, instead of the old vicious cycle of bad thoughts and unhealthy behavior encouraging each other on.

When you make a goal, you identify what you ultimately want to achieve and then assume that you will feel satisfied or happy once the goal has been achieved. Take a moment and think about how many people you know who are genuinely satisfied with their current lot in life. I know that even many of the people I know who are successful (by whatever parameters by which you define "success") aren't completely satisfied or happy. Some are even downright unhappy or depressed. We mistakenly assume that we are going to have to wait until we have met each and every goal to feel happy, that when we reach the pinnacle of health or achievement, our perspective will turn 180 degrees overnight.

The truth is that happiness comes slowly from a subtle shift of attitude, a shift of lifestyle, not from the numbers on a scale or notches in your belt. Just as you didn't become depressed or overweight in one step, you won't reverse it that way, either. The happiness, and all that comes with it, comes with each small goal attained. When I stepped on Meemaw's scale back in December of 2008, I told myself that I needed to lose 140 pounds. That was

the ultimate goal. But only two weeks later, I was already profoundly changed.

There was a cute photographer who worked with me on the university newspaper. I had been running and losing weight for a solid fifteen days or so, and was down fourteen or fifteen pounds. (It comes off quickly in the beginning.) Although fifteen pounds was only a very small percentage of the amount I had to lose and I didn't look noticeably different, I was already feeling the effects of my weight loss—an extra pep in my step, a new boost of confidence. My mentality had already changed drastically. Without doubting myself as I would have only two weeks prior or assuming that she would reject me, I asked her out on a date.

Her response didn't matter. (She politely declined.) What mattered was the change in me after only two weeks. I was grabbing life by the horns and doing it on my own terms. I was no longer sitting idly by. I still weighed more than Shaquille O'Neal, but my perspective had already undergone a complete makeover. I was confident where I had been timid. I was connecting with others where I had been a recluse. I was excited where I had been lethargic. *That's* what you have to look forward to when you change your life. And you won't be waiting long.

Only three months after I started running, Jed and I tackled a 10K. We were both feeling better than ever, and we wanted to bottle that feeling. Our way of doing this was to keep figuring out our next adventure and therefore keep setting the next goal. This kept our momentum going and kept us inspired and motivated every day. Each time we hit a new goal, we felt like celebrating. It gave us something to look forward to and a specific plan that we could count on.

Winter faded into spring and the racing season was at full throttle in central Arkansas by the time we set out to run our first 10K. Unlike at my first race, this time I had no hesitation about joining the other runners at the starting line. That's right—the *other* runners. I was truly one of them now. Only three months later, and I was a runner. I belonged. And that's how changing one thing can alter your view of yourself, your view of others, and your entire life.

As we got going, the energy in the crowd was palpable, and I found myself reflecting on the miles that had gotten me to that point. I was running smoothly this time, and my feet clapping the ground became a rhythmic metronome, the sound track to my thoughts. I had set and conquered many goals since starting to run. I was slimmer, sure, but here I was, tackling 6.2 miles after having been completely immobile just a hundred days prior. That's how I measured my success. I had no idea where I would be three months down the road, but it didn't matter yet. I wouldn't let that thought overwhelm me. The only thing of consequence was this moment. I was smiling, and that was enough for now. And if I could get to this point, I could break the hour mark. So I set a new goal for myself, and I pushed in order to get there.

The sun had risen and was doing its best to break us. Having done all my running up to that point in the cold, I found this a new obstacle. I gritted my teeth and focused my eyes on the goal. Had I looked down, I would have noticed two distinct red streaks running down my white cotton T-shirt. Apparently, when salt, water, cotton, and sensitive skin rub together for long enough, bad things can happen. Luckily, I was so focused on my immediate goal to break the hour mark that I didn't even feel it. (I certainly did feel it later, though, and there are simply no words for that level of pain.)

I pushed hard on mile four and the overexertion came back to bite me a little bit on mile five as my pace slowed to

PACING YOURSELF

around ten minutes per mile. Thankfully, I was so close to the finish line that mile six brought the adrenaline burst that I needed. The Capital City Classic is set up so that the finish area starts about half a mile from the actual finish line, giving the runners a much-needed shot of spectators and racers who had already finished cheering you in. I got on my horse and sprinted the final few hundred yards, breaking the hour mark with a finish time of 58:58. I had reached my goal.

"Dude . . . is that blood?" Jed was pointing at my chest. Before I could figure out why my chest was bleeding, he was doubled over in a fit of laughter. Other people noticed, too, and the looks of sympathy were enough to hint at the pain that was to come. Sure enough, it started to set in almost immediately and I had to walk carefully for about thirty-six hours to keep my shirt from coming back for more. It didn't bother me, though. I was elated. Shredded nipples or not, I had added another notch in the belt, had another distance down, and another goal had been met.

▶ READER QUESTION

"Ben, I'm too tired to run. What should I do?"

You wake up at six fifteen in the morning and the only thing that sounds appealing is hitting the snooze button and rolling over. This is very common, but also very beatable. First of all, you should have set a specific goal that specifies exactly what you need to do each day, each week, and each month. If you know that you need to run every other morning in order to reach your goal, you'll be a lot less likely to hit the snooze button.

So, no excuses—first, force your legs off the bed and sit up. If you get to the sitting position, you're one step closer. Now stand up. These two small steps will wake you up more than you think they will. Make yourself put on some shorts and shoes. Walk out of the bedroom and to the front porch or onto the street. Now start jogging. It's literally been roughly two and a half minutes, but think about exactly how much more awake you are already. The best trick to beating sleepiness is to move a little bit. Five minutes into your jog, you're going to be wide awake and your entire day will run exponentially smoother. As you go farther and hit more and more of your goals, running will ultimately refresh you, not tire you out.

The other trick seems obvious, but deserves a reminder. Get in bed thirty minutes earlier every night. Even if you're just lying there, you'll feel more rested in the morning. And a small cup of coffee ten minutes before a run never hurt anyone. Just remember this: you're not the only to deal with being tired. There are people out there who are running right now who are much sleepier than you. They're getting faster and living better while you're rolling over in bed. Don't sell yourself short. The feeling you'll get when you start reaching your goals will be so much more rewarding than a few more minutes of sleep.

Reader Testimonial

I lost a baby in 2009, became really depressed, and gained a lot of weight. I got myself up to 202 pounds and I'm only five-one. In January of 2010 I decided enough was enough. I saw that one of my friends was doing a triathlon and said, "What the hell?" I signed up for it, too. I trained my butt off (a lot of it, at least) and successfully completed

my first tri! It was so much fun. During that time, I also completed several 5Ks and five-mile runs.

What really transformed me was how much better I felt about myself and my health. I was able to be there for the child I already had. Through the urging of my trainer at the Y I belong to, I am now working on my personal trainer certification. I have lost over forty pounds and continue to train for events. In fact, I did a 5K this morning in 31:41, which is over six minutes faster than the one I did last year!

I can't wait to be able to help others reach their goals and better their lives when I get my certification! I have found my true calling in life, and I love that I set a good example for my daughter to exercise and stay healthy. I have even inspired a few of my friends to run, and that feels awesome!   *—Jennifer S*

10K TRAINING GUIDE

When you finish your first 5K, it's somewhat natural to begin thinking about a 10K. It is, after all, the next major milestone in the world of running. Yeah, there are a handful of 8Ks but the 10,000-meter is a classic.

The interesting thing about a 10K is that, for the most part, if you can run a 5K, you most likely can *get through* a 10K. Your fitness level is high enough that you could manage it. You might end up walk/jogging the last couple of miles, but you'll definitely finish if you attempt it. I don't recommend just winging it, though. You want your races to be memorable, and forgoing training is an easy way to kill your confidence at a race.

Ten kilometers truly is an easy distance to fall in love with. While there aren't as many 10Ks as 5Ks, you're still going to have plenty to choose from when you find your area's online race directory.

This guide is a beginner's plan, designed to help you do more than "just finish." It's designed under the assumption that, at minimum, you feel comfortable walking and jogging for twenty to thirty minutes and, more realistically, that you have done a 5K and feel confident at that distance.

On your long runs, you want to make sure that your pace is slow enough that you can easily hold a conversation or breathe through your nose. On your shorter midweek runs, you want to run a moderate pace, right around what you plan to run in the 10K race.

WEEK ONE

DAY ONE: run 2 miles

DAY TWO: rest, stretch

DAY THREE: run 2.5 miles

DAY FOUR: walk 40 minutes

DAY FIVE: rest

DAY SIX: run 3 miles

DAY SEVEN: walk 30 minutes

WEEK TWO

DAY ONE: run 2.25 miles

DAY TWO: rest, stretch

DAY THREE: run 2.5 miles

DAY FOUR: walk 40 minutes

DAY FIVE: rest

DAY SIX: run 3 miles

DAY SEVEN: walk 30 minutes

WEEK THREE

DAY ONE: run 2.5 miles

DAY TWO: rest, stretch

DAY THREE: run 2.75 miles

DAY FOUR: walk 40 minutes

DAY FIVE: rest

DAY SIX: run 3.5 miles

DAY SEVEN: walk 30 minutes

WEEK FOUR

DAY ONE: run 2.5 miles

DAY TWO: rest, stretch

DAY THREE: run 3 miles

DAY FOUR: run 1 mile, walk 20 minutes

DAY FIVE: rest

DAY SIX: run 4 miles

DAY SEVEN: jog 1 mile, walk 20 minutes

WEEK FIVE

DAY ONE: run 2.75 miles

DAY TWO: rest, stretch

DAY THREE: run 3.25 miles

DAY FOUR: run 1.5 miles, walk 20 minutes

DAY FIVE: rest

DAY SIX: run 4.5 miles

DAY SEVEN: jog 1 mile, walk 20 minutes

WEEK SIX

DAY ONE: run 3 miles

10k training guide

DAY TWO: rest, stretch

DAY THREE: run 3.5 miles

DAY FOUR: run 2 miles, walk 20 minutes

DAY FIVE: rest

DAY SIX: run 5 miles

DAY SEVEN: jog 2 miles

WEEK SEVEN

DAY ONE: run 3 miles

DAY TWO: rest, stretch

DAY THREE: run 3.5 miles

DAY FOUR: run 2.5 miles

DAY FIVE: rest

DAY SIX: run 6 miles

DAY SEVEN: walk 30 minutes

WEEK EIGHT

DAY ONE: run 3 miles

DAY TWO: rest, stretch

DAY THREE: run 2.5 miles

DAY FOUR: rest

DAY FIVE: rest

DAY SIX: RACE (or rest)

DAY SEVEN: RACE (or rest)

5

hitting the wall

IT'S PRETTY SCARY to start a whole new chapter of your life, whether it's the beginning of a weight-loss journey, a new job, or even a new relationship. First, there's the question of whether or not you'll be able to succeed. Can you do it? When you live an unlived life, you don't have to worry about failure. Every day is mundane and uninspired, but at least it's safe, it's comfortable, and it's easy. Truly living life is not easy. Life is hard. Life is scary. You might mess up. You might fail. You might get dumped, or fired, or injured, and risking each of these things takes confidence, trust, and bravery.

But the fear doesn't always rear its ugly head right away. You ask the girl out, go on your first run, or apply for a new job without hesitation, fueled by equal parts nerves and adrenaline. They get you through the first steps, and if you have good results, those effects will keep you going. It's not until the initial high dies down that the fear and doubt usually set in. This, of course, is called a rut.

Ruts are commonplace in every part of life and are a

natural consequence of running. When I was in second grade, I spent months begging my mom for a Game Boy. I've never been as desperate for something as I was for that digital box of black-and-white magic. All of the cool kids had one, and I just had to have one, too. My mom finally relented, and we loaded up into the van and headed out to the north Little Rock Toys "R" Us. I've never been so excited to get my hands on an electronic device, and I played the hell out of that bad boy for a solid three or four days straight. And then . . . it kind of lost its luster and I turned my attention to something else, something new.

It's natural to get excited about the start of something. Remember how amped up you would get before each new school year? I would get all the new gear—a new notebook to take a record-breaking amount of notes that year, new pens, new clothes, and a new backpack. Every year, I convinced myself that this was the year that I would stop procrastinating on my homework, study hard, and pull straight A's. And how long did it last—a week? A month? Two periods?

Most people get more excited about the *idea* of a new lifestyle than the new lifestyle itself. It's universal, and it applies to everything. The new job with the shiny new laptop and impressive new office is so incredibly exciting on your first day, but after a few weeks of endless meetings and an overflowing in-box, reality sets in and you realize that it's just another job. And no matter how many goals we set or how good of a start we get off to, the same thing happens when you're losing weight, starting a fitness journey, and mastering the art of running. The excitement eventually wears off. You see results and at some point think to yourself *This is good enough.*

It happens to all of us. In fact, you should start your journey knowing that you're eventually going to plateau so that you can anticipate it instead of being shocked when it happens to you. That way, you won't let it shake you. Hitting a rut or a plateau does not mean that you've failed or that you are even on the road to failure. Instead, the difference between success and failure lies in precisely what you do when you hit that rut. Do you get down on yourself, throw in the towel, and let all that good work go down the drain, or do you get back out there and keep on going?

When you hit a rut in your running, it can be for either physical or emotional reasons. If it's a physical rut, maybe you've been pushing too hard and need to rest more. Go back to basics. If the pounds have stopped falling off or you're not getting faster, it's probably because the same enthusiasm that was there in the beginning has waned. It's natural to start slacking or becoming content. Think back to what *exactly* you were doing in the beginning. Chances are that you were a lot more serious and were working harder then than you are now.

You have to find a way to attack life with the same enthusiasm. Start counting calories again, start a new training plan, and start tracking all your workouts. It's likely that you'll see that the intake of calories has increased and the output of energy has decreased, even if only slightly. Make a dramatic change. The reason you've found yourself on this plateau is that your habits have taken a slide to mediocrity because you're exhausted or lacking enthusiasm. Bust out of it by swearing off some of your vices. No more eating at restaurants for thirty days. No soda for three weeks. Do a 5K every weekend for three months.

Or, instead of going back to the beginning, push forward and do something newer and bigger than you've ever done before. Nothing will inspire you like making a commitment to doing something awesome—maybe even something that you're not entirely sure is possible. Sign up for a 5K. Grab a

HITTING THE WALL

friend and vow to do that half marathon that you've been thinking about. Better yet, join an actual running group and take it on with the support of a team. If it's more of a mental or an emotional rut, do not underestimate the importance of making running fun, or in this case, making it fun *again*. It's not something we naturally put together, fun and running, but it's the secret to keeping your new lifestyle going permanently.

healthy rewards for hitting a goal

TO KEEP YOURSELF motivated or put an end to a rut, make a game of it. Find ways to reward yourself that don't include celebrating with food or cigarettes or alcohol. Instead, vow to do it up healthy. The buddy (or team) system works so well for running in general, and also when it comes to rewarding yourself and staying motivated. Your running buddy should get you a reward when you hit a goal, and vice versa. This makes the whole thing more fun because your partner is right there in the trenches with you, and equally committed to helping you reach your goal. The resulting camaraderie will go a long way in helping you off that plateau.

Of course, you'll want to know how to finance these good-ies. You have to plan ahead for this. When you first start your journey (why not today?), buy a huge mason jar. Start by emp-tying your spare change into the jar every day. Then, every time you do something that you're proud of (hitting a goal, resisting the temptation of a five-dollar latte, forgoing McDonald's in favor of a healthy meal at home, or logging off Facebook and going for that run you've been putting off), stick a few dollars into the jar. Before long, you'll have accumulated enough extra money to pay for these healthy and motivating rewards. Here are some good ideas to get you started:

1. Get a massage

There's nothing better than a postrace massage to give your muscles and your mind some much-needed TLC.

2. Splurge on new clothes

After losing weight, there is nothing that feels better than buying new clothes that now fit and flatter you. Go to the mall and indulge in a reasonable shopping spree, and make sure to include a few pieces of new workout clothes to keep you motivated.

3. Combine a vacation with a getaway race

This is a great way to indulge in a guilt-free vacation and see a place that you might not otherwise get to. A bonus is that you won't undo all the good work that earned you the reward by boozing and eating it up throughout your vacation. You'll need to be on your A game for the race, so this will have to be a healthy but rewarding getaway.

4. Take a guilt-free sick day from work

Celebrate hitting your most recent goal by playing hooky. You deserve it.

5. Buy that new set of running shoes you've been eyeballing

This will also help you avoid the plateau that typically accompanies the inevitable comedown from the excitement of hitting a goal. You'll be motivated to stick with your training when you lace up those brand-new running shoes.

Emotional ruts can also happen when you get caught in the very thin line between healthy confidence and an overblown ego. If you've struggled with your weight as long

as I did, those first inklings of self-esteem can be addictive. They can make you feel invincible, which is definitely a good thing when you're running races and tackling new obstacles, but they can also be toxic.

My first running rut occurred in May of 2009, five months after I took that first jogging step. At this point in the journey, I was down about ninety pounds, and I was rocking the extra-large shirt and the size-38 jeans. I no longer hated the sight of my reflection in the mirror. The excitement and adrenaline of something new had carried me to this point, but the novelty had begun to fade. And the hole that the inspiration had left behind was quickly replaced by a sense of arrogance, a dangerous sense of entitlement. An "I" mentality had settled in my mind. *I* had done an amazing job. *I* had worked hard and the results were clear. This is all about *me.*

I was at the mall one day that May and I saw a girl *check me out.* That was something new to me. At 365 pounds, you don't exactly command attention every time you walk into a room. Well, that's not true; you do get a lot of attention, but it's usually in the form of quiet repulsion. The truth is that five months earlier, I would have assumed that this girl was looking at me in pity, but on this day, I believed that she was checking me out. That's how much my mentality had changed along with my body. I had gone from self-loathing and thinking I was repulsive to believing that this girl was looking at me *because I looked good.*

Whoa. That was cool.

But instead of motivating me even more, my overblown confidence was making me complacent. I was no longer in the journey for the right reasons. Just a few days earlier, Jed and I had signed up for a half marathon in Hot Springs, Arkansas. We were taking on 13.1 miles, and we had only a month to get ready for it. At that point, we were pretty confident with the 10K distance, and on May 31 we were going to try for the next big milestone.

But on May 25, I knew I wasn't going to be able to do it. This new attitude of mine had manifested itself in a horrible way. I wasn't running. I wasn't eating right. I was skipping the boot camp classes that Jed and I had signed up for. I was reverting to my old, unhealthy lifestyle—the McDonald's drive-through (still much too embarrassed to be seen inside), the twelve-hour sessions of sitting at the computer with my door locked, the skipping class . . . It was an oh-so-familiar lifestyle, but this time instead of self-hatred leading me there, it was a sense of pride and ego that was just as dangerous.

Back then, I truly believed that this was how weight-loss journeys worked. You do your thing for a few months, lose the weight, and then, magically, you are cured from your disease. You can now eat whatever you want, however much you want, go back to sitting on the couch for eighteen hours a day, and life will be perfect.

I called Jed and told him I wasn't going to be able to run the half. I just couldn't. I wasn't prepared. I had let a bad mind-set derail my five months of hard work. It was an embarrassing conversation, having to openly admit that I had fallen off the wagon. We had made a pact to do this together every step of the way, and he was disappointed in me. He had kept up his end of the bargain. He had done the training, done everything right, and here he was, losing his partner.

Even with my prideful mind-set, I knew that if I wasn't careful, I would crash and burn hard like I had so many times before. All the telltale signs of giving up were there—the lack of motivation, the reverting to bad habits, the hiding and retreating from life. This time it was my dad who wasn't going to let me fail.

HITTING THE WALL

Up to this point, Jed and I were doing this together every step of the way—the early morning boot camps, jogs around town, and grocery shopping for healthy foods. We were a team and it worked. We were closer than ever and enjoying the camaraderie that running brought us. My mom and dad were already divorced and were watching us from afar, each of them proud of the strides we were making in our lives, both literally and figuratively. My dad had enjoyed doing the adventure races with Jed, but had never expressed any interest in joining us in one of our races, so I had no idea that an appearance from him would ultimately be the thing to keep me on track.

"Ben," he said during one of our regular phone calls to catch up, "I've been secretly training along with you guys for this half marathon." He had no idea I had just given up on the idea. "I'm flying in this weekend. We're all running it together."

I couldn't tell him that I was giving up. How could I tell my father, who'd been training hard for weeks (like I should have been) not to come? I couldn't. "Yeah, man, come on down. It's going to be great." We hung up a few minutes later, and I knew right away that I couldn't let my dad down. I couldn't let my brother down, either. They were holding me accountable, whether I liked it or not. I was going to run this race even if it killed me. And it damn near did.

There I was, at mile seven of a thirteen-mile race, and the farthest I had ever run in my life was 6.2 miles. It was not a good place to be. I got mad—mad at myself for letting my arrogance blind me, mad at myself for not putting in the work that I knew I would so desperately need in this situation, mad at myself for going down the same path I had been down so many times before. But the confidence that I had gained over the past five months was still there underneath it all, and for the first time in my life, I used the anger at myself to do something positive. I was going to finish. Jed and Pa were there beside me, and I couldn't let them down. I couldn't let myself down. It would hurt, but I would finish.

And it did hurt. My feet were shredded from my lack of training calluses; my calves were screaming with every step; my quads were completely dead. It was like I was running on my skeleton instead of my muscles. I felt every pounding step.

But after two hours and thirty minutes of running through the hills in central Arkansas, I crossed the finish line, my body intact and my mind surprisingly spry.

Ruts are going to happen. How will you react? Plan for it now and you won't be able to fail. Plan your races in advance. Tell someone about each race you have planned, or better yet, sign up with a partner. Commit yourself. Push yourself off that plateau by aiming higher and higher, and there's no way that you'll be able to fall backward.

▶ READER QUESTION

"Ben, did you have any fears when you first started this journey?"

Yes, and looking back at the beginning of my journey now, I wonder why I had some uneasiness. When we're in this position—when we have something we need to change—I think we should be confident. Be excited. We have nothing to lose. We might have expectations, sure. Maybe we want to get to X weight or run X distance or give up X substance, and to miss would be disappointing, but if you can't get excited about changing your life and potentially inspiring others around you to do the same, you might need to check your pulse.

HITTING THE WALL

I was somewhere in the middle of the two extremes. I definitely had some fun unrealistic confidence. Once you start, your attitude about yourself changes. During the first few days, I felt like an elite runner and I was jogging at about a fifteen-minute-per-mile pace. My trick was to just go all out. At first I was (very) hesitant to take my shirt off at the local pool the first few times we did swim workouts. It's not every day you see a 365-pound guy swimming laps like he's Michael Phelps, but that's what I was doing. And it was liberating. I know, though, that not everyone feels the confidence.

Sometimes it's not just a lack of confidence; it's a full-blown phobia—a huge source of anxiety.

When I think about fears and starting journeys, I always (and will always) think of Nancy. In the summer of 2011, the Do Life Movement (the organization/community that my father, brother, and I started) did a thirty-two-city 5K tour across the U.S. and Canada. We toured nonstop for forty days in a van covering twelve thousand miles. When we rolled into Buffalo, New York, though, I ran with one of the most inspiring women I've ever met.

For the first mile and a half, I ran alongside Nancy. She was overweight, a beginning runner, and we were at the back of the pack together. She told me she had started only eleven weeks beforehand. When we announced the tour, she knew she wanted to join us and began training. But Nancy was overcome with anxiety when it came to running outside in public. It's a common thing to feel uncomfortable working out in front of people—I know I felt a little uneasy running outside at 350 pounds.

Nancy told me that the nerves were so prevalent that she ran inside. I assumed that meant she bought a treadmill. No, Nancy literally trained by running through her house, from room to room, every day, in anticipation of the 5K.

We were at mile two when she began to struggle. "I really want to break fifty minutes," she said. I looked at my GPS to calculate our pace. I was a little skeptical. We could do it, but she was going to have to keep at it. And she did.

Eventually, we turned the corner and the finish line came into sight. Sweat poured from her brow and she limped into each stride while still maintaining a jog. We finished in forty-nine minutes flat; she had beaten her goal.

She went from not being able to run at all to finishing those 3.1 scorching-hot miles. And she did so in front of forty other Do Lifers who were there to scream and clap in excitement as she crossed the finish line. When I told everyone it was her first 5K ever, they cheered even louder.

And that's exactly what fears can become—victories. Fears, ruts, and plateaus are all the same. Each of them provides us with an opportunity to either give up or keep pushing and overcome them. It's your choice. I vote with Nancy.

Reader Testimonial

The last day of spring break 2010, I made the decision to do something about my life. I started running and working out to get healthy and make a better life for myself, my wife, and our twin daughters. I had just turned thirty and didn't want to spend my thirties like I did my twenties. After going laps around the track many nights without

feeling like I was going to die, I started to develop a passion for running. I set a goal to do a 5K turkey trot. I went from 269 pounds at the end of spring break to 169 pounds in just eight months—a hundred pounds lost! Two months later, I did my first 10K, and I ran several 5Ks and 10Ks in 2011. In February of 2012, my wife and I did our first half marathon, and in February of 2013 we'll do our first full marathon.

In the middle of my journey, I came across your "My 120 Journey" video on YouTube and I think that really helped me keep going. I love wearing my "Do Life" T-shirt out and about, because I feel like I'm representing a new me! Thanks, Ben! —Jared R

HALF MARATHON
TRAINING GUIDE

The half marathon is such a great distance. It's long enough to include "marathon" in the name, but still has a training plan that leaves room for a social life. A half marathon, when run in conjunction with a full marathon, typically outsells the full simply because it's a much more "fun" distance.

This twelve-week guide is designed under the assumption that you feel comfortable running a few miles with ease. If you don't feel confident running three or four miles a couple of times per week, try a 5K or 10K first.

The world record for a half marathon is fifty-eight minutes and twenty-three seconds, held by Zersenay Tadese of Eritrea in Africa. For a little perspective, that puts him at running four minutes and twenty-seven seconds per mile for 13.1 miles or 13.5 miles per hour. If I *sprint* fifty yards or so, I can just barely hit 13.5 miles per hour, and the elites can maintain it for nearly an hour. It's probably best if you don't attempt that pace. Don't worry; most people run the half marathon in anywhere from two to three hours.

Here are some terms you should know for this training plan:

> ▶ **Easy run:** More of a "jog" than a run. During your easy runs, you should be able to hold a conversation and breathe through your nose. Pace is roughly ninety to 120 seconds slower per mile than your planned marathon pace.

▶ **Tempo:** Should be comfortably uncomfortable. Push yourself during tempo runs, but not as fast as, say, your 5K race pace. Aim for forty-five to sixty seconds faster per mile than your planned marathon pace.

▶ **Moderate:** Just as it sounds. Run at whatever pace feels comfortable. Not easy but not tempo. During my moderate runs I aim for right around marathon pace, but don't beat myself up if it's a little slower.

▶ **Cross:** Cross-training. Substitute bike, swim, yoga, or whatever other cardio discipline you please.

This is a beginner's half marathon training guide, so we're going to stay away from hill workouts and focus on getting the miles under our belts. If, though, you want to push yourself a little further, every two weeks swap out a midweek run for a nice thirty-minute or hour-long hill workout.

WEEK ONE

DAY ONE: 3 easy miles

DAY TWO: cross 30 minutes

DAY THREE: 3 easy miles

DAY FOUR: 2.5 tempo miles, 15-minute walk

DAY FIVE: rest

DAY SIX: 3 easy miles

DAY SEVEN: 2 easy miles, or walk

WEEK ONE TOTAL: 13.5 miles

WEEK TWO

DAY ONE: 3 easy miles

DAY TWO: cross 30 minutes

DAY THREE: 3 moderate miles

DAY FOUR: 3.5 tempo miles

DAY FIVE: rest

DAY SIX: 4 easy miles

DAY SEVEN: 2 easy miles, or walk

WEEK TWO TOTAL: 15.5 miles

WEEK THREE

DAY ONE: 3 moderate miles

DAY TWO: cross 30 minutes

DAY THREE: 3 moderate miles

DAY FOUR: 4 tempo miles

DAY FIVE: rest

DAY SIX: 5 easy miles

DAY SEVEN: 2 easy miles, or walk

WEEK THREE TOTAL: 17 miles

half marathon training guide

WEEK FOUR

DAY ONE: 3 moderate miles

DAY TWO: cross 30 minutes

DAY THREE: 4 moderate miles

DAY FOUR: 4 tempo miles

DAY FIVE: rest

DAY SIX: 5.5 easy miles

DAY SEVEN: 2 easy miles, or walk

WEEK FOUR TOTAL: 18.5 miles

WEEK FIVE

DAY ONE: 3 moderate miles

DAY TWO: cross 30 minutes

DAY THREE: 4 moderate miles

DAY FOUR: 5 tempo miles

DAY FIVE: rest

DAY SIX: 6 easy miles

DAY SEVEN: 2 easy miles, or walk

WEEK FIVE TOTAL: 20 miles

WEEK SIX

DAY ONE: 3 moderate miles

DAY TWO: cross 30 minutes

DAY THREE: 4 moderate miles

DAY FOUR: 5.5 tempo miles

DAY FIVE: rest

DAY SIX: 6.5 easy miles

DAY SEVEN: 2 easy miles, or walk

WEEK SIX TOTAL: 21 miles

WEEK SEVEN

DAY ONE: 3 moderate miles

DAY TWO: cross 30 minutes

DAY THREE: 5 moderate miles

DAY FOUR: 6 tempo miles

DAY FIVE: rest

DAY SIX: 7 easy miles

DAY SEVEN: 2 easy miles, or walk

WEEK SEVEN TOTAL: 23 miles

WEEK EIGHT

DAY ONE: 3 moderate miles

DAY TWO: cross 30 minutes

DAY THREE: 5 moderate miles

DAY FOUR: 6 tempo miles

DAY FIVE: rest

half marathon training guide

DAY SIX: 8 easy miles

DAY SEVEN: 2 easy miles, or walk

WEEK EIGHT TOTAL: 24 miles

WEEK NINE

DAY ONE: 3 moderate miles

DAY TWO: cross 30 minutes

DAY THREE: 5.5 moderate miles

DAY FOUR: 6 tempo miles

DAY FIVE: rest

DAY SIX: 9.5 easy miles

DAY SEVEN: 2 easy miles, or walk

WEEK NINE TOTAL: 26 miles

WEEK TEN

DAY ONE: 3 moderate miles

DAY TWO: cross 30 minutes

DAY THREE: 4 moderate miles

DAY FOUR: 4 tempo miles

DAY FIVE: rest

DAY SIX: 10.5 easy miles

DAY SEVEN: 2 easy miles, or walk

WEEK TEN TOTAL: 23.5 miles

WEEK ELEVEN

DAY ONE: 3 moderate miles

DAY TWO: cross 30 minutes

DAY THREE: 4 moderate miles

DAY FOUR: 3 tempo miles

DAY FIVE: rest

DAY SIX: 11 easy miles

DAY SEVEN: 2 easy miles, or walk

WEEK ELEVEN TOTAL: 23 miles

WEEK TWELVE

DAY ONE: 3 easy miles

DAY TWO: rest

DAY THREE: 3 easy miles

DAY FOUR: 2 easy miles (or rest)

DAY FIVE: rest

DAY SIX: rest or half marathon

DAY SEVEN: rest or half marathon

WEEK TWELVE TOTAL: 21.1 miles

half marathon training guide

turning the corner

I **F YOU'VE HIT** a rut or fallen off track, there are a million tricks and techniques that you can use to get back on the wagon and find a new spark. But at the end of the day, you just have to do it. Get back out there, start back at the beginning, and the rut will pass quickly. You have to find a way to push yourself beyond what you're currently doing. Go bigger. Find a reason to push further. Don't wait for someone to come and save you like my dad saved me by holding me accountable. I was lucky. You might not be. You have to force *yourself* off the plateau.

Don't sit around and worry that you'll never get your mojo back. Trust that it's going to happen. Simply buckle down and push harder than you've been pushing. Get mad and get strong. Use your frustration and disappointment in yourself to your own benefit. You'll be surprised by what you can accomplish by harnessing some of that anger. Go prove yourself wrong when you doubt that you can do it. Look at yourself and figure out why you're stuck. Are you living on someone else's terms? Are you letting others define your successes and failures? Forget them. You know what you need to do, and you have to do it on your own terms. Take it back. Regain control. The rest will follow.

As I hugged my dad and brother there at the finish line of the half marathon and then winced my way back to the car, I had an epiphany. Suddenly, I realized that this wasn't about me. Everything—this whole journey—wasn't about me or about girls at the mall who may or may not have been checking me out. This wasn't about flirty messages on Facebook, or even the way I felt about my reflection in the mirror. This journey was about life. It was (and still is) about happiness, the same happiness that Meemaw had asked me about on Christmas Eve.

My perspective shifted in an instant, and that's what it takes sometimes. So take a moment now and think about what this is (and isn't) all about for you. In that moment, I realized that this is not about weight loss; it's about being a healthy person. It's not about running; it's about improving yourself and finding ways to quantify that. It's not about finishing a race; it's about pushing yourself and seeing just how far you can go. It's not about results; it's about the journey. It's about reversing the negative cycles of the past and replacing them with thoughts and actions that will do good things for not just you, but everyone around you.

For me, running filled the void that had previously been occupied by unhealthy food, a sedentary life, and ill-advised casino trips. Now I pass a casino three or four times a week during my runs, but I'm never tempted to break out the credit cards and sit down at the blackjack tables the same way I am when, say, I'm up late at night secretly giving in to my insatiable desire for a McChicken sandwich (or three).

You have to act your way into right thinking, but not just in one area of life. Unhealthy actions in one part of your life will breed negative thoughts and unhealthy behaviors in all parts of your life. This was true for me, and it's true for most people with a weight or addiction problem. But positive, healthy behaviors can spread like wildfire, too—not just throughout your own life, but into the lives of others. I recently saw my friend Guy running through town in the dead of winter with his new girlfriend. Perhaps I'm rubbing off on him. I hope I am. When you break a habit, when you give up your vices, it's imperative to fill those voids with something positive. If you don't, your time becomes idle and you quickly slip back to the things you know—the things that are easy and comfortable.

After the race, Jed, Pa, and I went to celebrate at a local burger joint. I slurped a peanut butter milk shake as we rehashed the race, how we had done, what sucked, and what didn't. The aroma of french fries drifted throughout the diner as we figured out where we were headed from here. It became clear that this wasn't a one-off for Pa. He wanted to join our team, to do these races alongside his two sons, and we were thrilled to have him join us. It was no longer Pa and Jed doing exciting things together while I was left out. It was the three of us now. I was a member of the team.

The question that had kept us going throughout this journey was eventually voiced. "What's next?" A fire had been relit in my motivation. The rut was over. The plateau was history. I had found an escape from the rut and a spark had been ignited. Together, we set our new goal—the marathon. Those 26.2 miles had been on our minds for a few months, but we wanted to work our way up to it before we jumped into the maniacal world of marathon training. But now, with my having felt how close I came to sliding all the way backward, was no time to wait. I was still recovering from the half marathon when Jed called me with a plan.

"Dude," he said. "We're doing a triathlon."

Here we go, I thought. "All right," I told him. "When is it?"

"This Saturday."

I never said we did any of this the "right" way, and I wouldn't necessarily recommend going about any of this exactly the same way that we did. But the truth is that in life, there is never one right way. Everyone has their own version of what the "right" way is. For some, it might mean living by the book, precisely planning out each step. For others, it might mean living moment to moment, never even thinking a step in advance. It doesn't matter which tack you take. All that matters is that you do it by your own rules. This is your life—your one and only life. Are you going to live it by someone else's rules, or write your own?

Jed and I had decided at the beginning that we weren't going to play by anyone else's rules. We had run a 5K only days after our first run. I had just run a half marathon with basically no training at all. But I had done it. The same goes for you. Don't follow my path. Create your own. Train as much as your body needs. Push yourself to your own limits, not mine or anyone else's. I was finally living my life on my own terms and finding the smile that I had searched so long for, and I certainly wasn't going to stop now.

But, still, a triathlon . . . that's a five-hundred-meter swim, fifteen-mile bike ride, and 3.1-mile run. I rarely rode my bike, and I had swum a few times at the fitness center pool, but had never done a lake swim. I had never practiced transitioning from one discipline to the other. None of this mattered. Once again, we dove in, but this time literally. Only a few days later, we found ourselves on the sandy shores of Beaverfork Lake in some unfortunate spandex and borrowed goggles, ready to take on our first tri.

Bikes: This seems obvious, right? It's a bike. What could there possibly be to know? The answer is: a lot. First, which type of bike will you use—road bike or mountain bike? Road bikes are much more convenient, speedy, and lightweight than mountain bikes, but cost a little more. Mountain bikes are rugged, heavy, more stable, and will handle most types of terrain. Your first time on a road bike will likely feel a little tense. There is no give in a road bike—no shocks—it's a very rigid experience. You'll be fine to compete in a shorter-distance race with a mountain bike if it helps you feel more at ease, but if you're at all serious about triathlons, a road bike is an investment you'll want to make.

Brick Workout: A brick is any training exercise that combines two disciplines back to back. Most commonly, it will put the two distances that go with each other—swim/bike or bike/run—but I've done my fair share of swim/runs, too. Bricks are imperative to get you used to the sensation that comes from transitioning from one sport to the next.

Transition: During your triathlon, there will be areas for you to transition between the different courses, named, appropriately, transition areas or T1 (swim-to-bike transition) and T2 (bike-to-run transition). You will drop all your gear off at transition areas prior to the race (either the night before or morning of) to make the transitions as smooth and speedy as possible. T1 will hold your bike, most importantly, your helmet, and shoes, but put other helpful stuff there as you need it: towel, change of clothes, sunscreen—anything that you think you might require to get you on the road prepared.

Clipless Pedals: If you've ever seen a serious cyclist spinning through town, chances are they were wearing those odd-looking shoes that click when they walk. Ninety-five percent of the competitors at triathlons will be wearing these shoes. They clip into the pedal, giving the rider a more powerful spin cadence. (This way the rider is pulling up while simultaneously pushing with the other foot, something not possible with standard pedals.) I will say, however, that in my five triathlons and years of training, I've never used a pair, so don't fret if you don't want to pony up the two-hundred-dollars-plus for special pedals and shoes, particularly if you're looking at the shorter triathlons.

Open Water Swim: Exactly as it sounds. This means you go to your local lake, river, or ocean, hop in, and do your training swim. Swimming in the open water is much different from swimming at your local YMCA, and you need to feel comfortable doing it so that you don't have a panic attack when you are in thirty-feet-deep water three hundred yards from shore. Many people tie a rope to their waist dragging a flotation device ten or fifteen feet behind them in case anything happens while they're training alone.

Wet Suit: Wet suits will make your swimming life a living dream. For one, you'll be more hydrodynamic, cutting through the water at lightning speed. For two, wet suits provide some buoyancy, keeping you on top of the water, making your strokes a little more efficient, and, you know, helping you not drowning. For Olympic distances and up, I say wet suits are a very wise investment. Wet suits are, however, only legal in water temperatures below seventy-eight degrees, so plan accordingly.

Goggles: You need them.

Vaseline: Lube up those nips, fellas.

It was early June, but at seven a.m. the water was still chilly to the touch, so we waded out a little bit with a couple of hundred other triathletes to warm up. They all looked much more qualified than us, and I noticed this at the time, but by now it didn't shake me. I was one of them. Finishing the tri didn't even matter, and my time certainly didn't matter at all. What mattered was that I was addicted to this new life and I was really living it. I had shown up, and I would give it my all. That's what made me one of them, and that thought made me smile.

The biggest issue with competing in your first triathlon is that, no matter what, you can't train for sharing a smallish water path with hundreds (or thousands) of other swimmers. As the gun blasted, I received my own initiation into the world of triathlons with a nice swift kick to the face. If you're serious about entering the world of triathlon, you must first learn to accept that you will, at some point, get jarred with an open hand, foot, elbow, knee, or some other flailing body part. Luckily, I feel reasonably comfortable in deep open water, so I just adjusted my dislodged goggles and kept on trucking, and after thirteen minutes of choppy swimming, I jogged to the transition area.

The feeling of your full weight after a high-energy weightless workout makes for some odd jogging, but after a couple of minutes in transition, I was on my bike, spinning my way through the course. I knew those fifteen miles would take an hour, maybe a little more, so I settled in and spun the pedals in a slower but efficient pace.

TURNING THE CORNER

The sun was peeking out now and the temperature was headed north; the sweat that formed under my helmet dripped into my eyes every so often. My legs began to tire halfway through, and my mind drifted to thoughts of how I was going to hold up during the 5K run. It didn't help that I was still a little tight from running the half marathon a week before on poor training. But one thing that races like these will teach you is to live in the moment. The minute you start worrying about the next leg of the journey is the same minute you falter. Are you going now? Okay, then keep going. Of course, the exact same principle can be applied to every part of life. You can't worry about the future, or it will make you falter right now. I tried to banish thoughts of the run from my mind, but the fear was tripping me up a little.

Sure enough, as I finished the bike section and stepped down to start running, my legs felt like lead—too heavy to move, much less run. But I tried. I pushed. I focused on putting one foot in front of the other, and after a quarter of a mile or so, my legs finally relented. The heaviness from the bike ride was gone, and I was surprisingly fresh to finish up the race. A week after my first half marathon, I had done my first tri. Another goal had been met.

▶ READER QUESTION

"Ben, do you need to be an experienced swimmer and biker before you start training for a triathlon?"

No. I'll put it this way—when I signed up for my first triathlon, I didn't own a bike and had swum a very minimal amount and with no proper lessons or coaching. That's the thing—we jump into these things—whatever they may be—not because we're ready for them, but because they excite and intrigue us. We may be scared, but we're also determined, and that can go a long way. That said, you do need to prepare for these races in order to avoid injury. So buy or borrow a bike, and jump into the local pool. Just try it. Slowly, you'll get comfortable. You'll be surprised by how far your natural ability will take you if you just jump in and keep going, little by little.

Then, once you're comfortable in the water and on the bike and you feel like you need it, go ahead and get some proper help. Ask lots of questions. Watch videos. Do whatever you need to do. But don't let the anxiety you feel about something keep you from trying it. That anxious, excited feeling is the exact reason that you should try it, anyway. It'll be worth it to see how much better you get and how likely you are to succeed.

Reader Testimonial

Many times I think about that moment when I said, "Enough is enough." I climbed a mesa in Oklahoma nearly three years ago, and that was the spark that lit the fire inside me. I did it! I've lost a total of about two hundred pounds, but it's not what I've lost . . . it's what I've gained. I gained and strengthened so many of my friendships. I learned to love myself for who I am, no matter how much I weigh. I fell in love with running. I've run too many 5Ks to count, two half marathons, and a Tour de Pain Extreme in twenty-four hours. I am now a personal trainer and hope to help others, to pay it forward. —Lisa B

SPRINT TRIATHLON TRAINING GUIDE

So you might wanna try a tri, eh? Get excited, because the triathlon is some of the most fun you'll ever have. It's tough, no doubt, and you're going to need to train. But there's something so incredibly satisfying about conquering a multisport event that standard running races just don't offer.

First and foremost, the thing you need to understand is that triathlons are doable. Many people are turned off because when they hear the word *triathlon*, the image that pops into their mind is the Ironman Championships in Hawaii on NBC. Don't freak out; triathlons come in many shapes and sizes, just like the competitors in them. You're going to learn many new terms throughout this guide—it might feel a little overwhelming, but when all's said and done, remember this: it's just another race. You can swim, bike, and run; all you have to do is do them back to back to back. Do the training, get comfortable doing the individual sports, pace yourself, and you'll be fine.

There are some downsides to triathlons—they are more expensive, both in racing fees and in equipment. Whereas in running all you really need is a decent set of shoes (and now with the popularity of minimalist running, not even those), in triathlon you're going to, at the very least, need a bike, riding helmet, and some goggles. Some optional items include a wet suit, tri suit, clipless pedals, a bike computer, and on and on and on. There really is a market for just about anything in the world of triathlon; people want to go faster and farther and are willing to spend lots of money to do so. But let's not get too caught up in all the fancy stuff. My goal for this guide is to get you familiar with the sport, encourage you to take it on, and help you train for your first one.

The first step to doing your triathlon is figuring out what distance you want to take on. Triathlons come in a few major standard categories. Some of your local triathlons might not be the exact distances listed, but most will be close.

Super Sprint Distance: The shortest standard distance in triathlon. This is quite rare, or raced in conjunction with a longer tri.

> 400-meter swim
> 10K (6.2-mile) bike
> 2.5K (1.5-mile) run

This is a perfect triathlon if you want to get your feet wet before tackling bigger distances. The super sprint will require a much lower-volume training guide and will help you get comfortable doing the disciplines in a race situation.

Sprint Distance: Probably the most popular triathlon distance. Short enough for beginners to aim for and feel comfortable with and lots of fun for seasoned vets to speed through. This is the race that this training guide will prepare you for.

> 750-meter (.46-mile) swim (although many races make it an even half mile (800 meters)

Sprint triathlon training guide

20K (12.4-mile) bike
5K (3.1-mile) run

The sprint triathlon is going to require only three to five hours per week of training, so you're not going to have to give up your social life (like you will have to when you do an Ironman . . .)

Olympic Distance: My personal favorite distance.

1,500-meter (0.93-mile) swim
40K (24.8-mile) bike
10K (6.2-mile) run

The only triathlon I've done twice is the Showman Shooter Triathlon just east of Memphis—it's an Olympic distance. Olympics are for those looking for a little more challenge than a sprint, but are still very doable for a first-time triathlete. Finishes are going to be anywhere from two to four hours, so you're going to need to amp up training if you want to take on the distance, but it's worth it and it's the most fun I've had at a triathlon.

Half Iron Distance: And now we're approaching the crazy folks. The half iron distance is sometimes called the 70.3, the sum total of the miles involved.

1.2-mile swim
56-mile bike
13.1-mile run

Obviously, the 70.3 is not intended for the beginner triathlete, but don't let that scare you when aiming for one; just get some smaller races under your belt. Take one summer to get a feel for the sport and start looking at Half Irons in the New Year.

As I mentioned before, this is a beginner's sprint-distance guide. You should feel comfortable walking/running a 5K before taking on this plan. It's a twelve-week guide, though, so even if you're just starting, this guide will take you to the starting line with confidence. Each workout will be given in minutes rather than miles. Remember—quality over quantity. Swim, bike, and run at a comfortable pace. It's fine to do your swim workouts in a pool, but make sure it's at least a twenty-five-yard pool and that you aren't kicking off too hard on the walls. You want to emphasize stroking your way through the water, not how far you can go without actually swimming. There will be three open water swims in the guide; I recommend making all three, but definitely try to get into the open water at least twice.

WEEK ONE

DAY ONE: run 20 minutes, walk 10 minutes

DAY TWO: swim 20 minutes

DAY THREE: bike 20 minutes

DAY FOUR: run 20 minutes, walk 10 minutes

DAY FIVE: rest

DAY SIX: bike 30 minutes, run 15 minutes

DAY SEVEN: swim 20 minutes

WEEK ONE TOTAL: 165 minutes

WEEK TWO

DAY ONE: run 25 minutes

DAY TWO: swim 25 minutes

DAY THREE: bike 20 minutes, walk 10 minutes

DAY FOUR: swim 20 minutes, bike 20 minutes

DAY FIVE: rest

DAY SIX: bike 50 minutes

DAY SEVEN: run 20 minutes

WEEK TWO TOTAL: 190 minutes

WEEK THREE

DAY ONE: swim 20 minutes

DAY TWO: bike 35 minutes

DAY THREE: run 25 minutes, walk 10 minutes

DAY FOUR: run 20 minutes, swim 15 minutes

DAY FIVE: rest

DAY SIX: bike 30 minutes, run 20 minutes

DAY SEVEN: swim 25 minutes open water

WEEK THREE TOTAL: 200 minutes

WEEK FOUR

DAY ONE: run 25 minutes

DAY TWO: bike 40 minutes

DAY THREE: swim 20 minutes

DAY FOUR: bike 30 minutes, run 15 minutes

DAY FIVE: rest

DAY SIX: swim 20 minutes

DAY SEVEN: run 30 minutes, walk 20 minutes

WEEK FOUR TOTAL: 200 minutes

WEEK FIVE

DAY ONE: bike 30 minutes

DAY TWO: swim 20 minutes

DAY THREE: run 25 minutes, walk 20 minutes

DAY FOUR: bike 30 minutes

DAY FIVE: rest

DAY SIX: bike 30 minutes, run 25 minutes

DAY SEVEN: rest

WEEK FIVE TOTAL: 180 minutes

WEEK SIX (easy week)

DAY ONE: run 15 minutes

DAY TWO: swim 15 minutes

sprint triathlon training guide

TURNING THE CORNER

DAY THREE: rest

DAY FOUR: bike 20 minutes

DAY FIVE: rest

DAY SIX: walk 30 minutes

DAY SEVEN: swim 20 minutes

WEEK SIX TOTAL: 100 minutes

WEEK SEVEN

DAY ONE: run 20 minutes

DAY TWO: swim 25 minutes

DAY THREE: bike 25 minutes

DAY FOUR: run 30 minutes

DAY FIVE: rest

DAY SIX: bike 50 minutes

DAY SEVEN: swim 20 minutes open water

WEEK SEVEN TOTAL: 170 minutes

WEEK EIGHT

DAY ONE: run 40 minutes

DAY TWO: swim 25 minutes

DAY THREE: bike 35 minutes, walk 15 minutes

DAY FOUR: run 25 minutes

DAY FIVE: rest

DAY SIX: bike 40 minutes, run 20 minutes

DAY SEVEN: swim 15 minutes

WEEK EIGHT TOTAL: 215 minutes

WEEK NINE

DAY ONE: run 40 minutes

DAY TWO: run 30 minutes

DAY THREE: swim 20 minutes

DAY FOUR: bike 50 minutes

DAY FIVE: rest

DAY SIX: bike 40 minutes, run 25 minutes

DAY SEVEN: swim 20 minutes

WEEK NINE TOTAL: 225 minutes

WEEK TEN

DAY ONE: run 45 minutes

DAY TWO: bike 45 minutes, run 15 minutes

DAY THREE: swim 20 minutes

DAY FOUR: bike 60 minutes

DAY FIVE: rest

DAY SIX: run 50 minutes

DAY SEVEN: swim 25 minutes open water

WEEK TEN TOTAL: 260 minutes

sprint triathlon training guide

WEEK ELEVEN (taper week)

DAY ONE: run 25 minutes

DAY TWO: bike 20 minutes, run 20 minutes

DAY THREE: swim 20 minutes

DAY FOUR: run 20 minutes

DAY FIVE: rest

DAY SIX: swim 20 minutes

DAY SEVEN: swim 10 minutes

WEEK ELEVEN TOTAL: 135 minutes

WEEK TWELVE

DAY ONE: run 15 minutes

DAY TWO: bike 20 minutes

DAY THREE: swim 20 minutes

DAY FOUR: rest

DAY FIVE: rest

DAY SIX: jog 10 minutes

DAY SEVEN: RACE!

WEEK TWELVE TOTAL: 65 minutes (plus race time)

testing yourself

IT'S ONE THING to talk about goals being specific and quantitative, which is, of course, extremely important. But your goals—no matter what area of life they're in—have to progress throughout your journey with exactly the right slope and rhythm. If your goals are too far apart, too great a jump from one to another, you're setting yourself up for failure. You can't go from a 5K to a marathon, for instance, without hitting at least a few medium-sized races in between. I didn't necessarily pace myself as much as I should have in the beginning, and it's important for you to set more realistic goals for yourself that progress at the right rate.

This goes for any type of goal in life, not just in running, but the opposite is also true. If your goals plateau, so will your progress, and your mind-set right along with it. The answer is to keep pushing yourself harder and harder, in a rhythm that makes you feel inspired rather than exhausted and burned-out. You'll never know what you're capable of achieving next if you never test yourself.

Having completed the triathlon, we naturally shifted our sights to the marathon. It was the perfect next step for me—a way of pushing and testing myself that certainly wasn't going to be easy, but at that point didn't seem impossible, either. I was becoming more of an experienced runner now (a real runner), and so I knew what qualities to look for in a marathon. It had to be in a cool city. Pa, Jed, and I had to do it together, so the timing of the marathon had to work with all of our personal and training schedules. If we tried to tackle it too soon, it would become an unrealistic goal. If we waited too long, we'd lose our momentum. It was now June, and we predicted that our training would take four months, so we began looking for October marathons. Within just a few hours, we settled on the Denver marathon on October 18. The bar had been raised and I was psyched.

the original marathon

ACCORDING TO LEGEND, the origins of the marathon dates back to 490 BC in ancient Greece, where a Greek messenger named Pheidippides ran twenty-five miles from Marathon to Athens to announce Greece's victory in the battle of Marathon. Unfortunately, just after announcing the good news, he died immediately. (He had allegedly also run 150 miles two days beforehand.) The marathon went on to become one of the original Olympic events in 1896.

Marathon training is different from training for other distances in that the standard training guides only take you up to twenty or twenty-one miles. The reason for this is that any fitness or cardio benefits that come from running longer while training are countered by the toll it takes on your body and the time that it takes to recover from running that long.

In other words, it will interrupt your training to run that far before the actual race. Besides, they say that if you can go twenty miles, you can go 26.2. This is why marathons are such a great way to test yourself—because you truly don't know whether or not you can do it until you actually do it. As a result, the sense of accomplishment that you feel after the fact is much greater than with other races, when you've already run that distance a hundred times beforehand.

Before I knew anything about running, I believed that there were marathon runners and then there were "normal" runners, and that there was a wide schism between the two that could never be filled. In other words, I thought that you were born a marathoner, not that you became one. I was wrong. The difference between marathon runners and regular runners is exactly the same as the difference between runners and nonrunners, and that is simply running and how far you run.

It's important to know that the marathon is a reachable goal, but it is a serious commitment. You have to set goals for yourself along the way to this bigger goal. First there's a fifteen-mile run, followed by a sixteen-mile run, and then seventeen-, eighteen-, nineteen-, and twenty-mile runs. After you've been training for a few weeks, you forget that days have their own names and meanings to the rest of the world, and start thinking in twenty-four-hour chunks of running. The mail isn't delivered on recovery short-run day. T.G.I.R.D. Thank God it's rest day.

Even though we didn't all live near each other, training alongside Jed and Pa for the marathon not only kept me on target, reaching each individual goal as it came, but made the training fun. We competed with each other throughout, texting each other our training times and daily caloric intakes, smack talking, and doing whatever it took

to motivate each other to do the miles. We had become a team, taking on these challenges together, and as a team we learned how to get the best performance from ourselves and each other.

Together, slowly but surely, we got better. We went farther. We sweat buckets, we chafed nipples, and even peed a little blood, but we did get better. (I found out later that blood in the urine is a side effect of dehydration. If your pee starts to look like Kool-Aid, just modify yourself accordingly and make sure to stay hydrated.) It's important to understand that running becomes exponentially easier throughout this whole process. The seven miles that once seemed impossible eventually becomes an "easy run." I know so many people who have given up on running because it's so tough at first—and it is. It's incredible, though, how quickly it becomes less miserable and how it eventually becomes surprisingly enjoyable.

ben's do life marathon commandments

1. Adhere to the guide.

The training guide at the end of this chapter is based on my own training, marathon plans from my past that have worked for me, advice from my personal trainer, and common sense. These things work. They are tried-and-true. If you stick to them and are strict about it, you will finish the marathon. You simply have to get the miles in. You can't fake a marathon, so don't try.

2. However, don't freak out if you miss a run, or even two runs.

Just pick back up and get back on the plan. If you happen to miss a long, easy run, make it up. Your long, easy runs have to get into the bank one way or the other.

3. Hydrate and fuel.

This goes for both training and the actual race. Make sure to increase your water intake. A good rule of thumb is to take your weight and divide it in half. That's the number of ounces of water that you should be drinking per day (with a minimum of seventy to eighty ounces). Try to plan runs that go past water fountains, carry your own water, or else carry some cash and stop by a gas station to buy bottles. On your long runs, head out an hour before you start and hide bottles of water or sports drinks every few miles.

Also, don't be afraid to pack a sports gel packet like GU to keep fueled. Most marathons have aid stations every mile that should be at least stocked with water and usually a sports drink. Drink when you feel thirsty, being careful not to overdo it. (You don't want to be sloshing through your race.) Typically, I make sure to get some liquid every mile even if I don't drink the entire cup. A swallow or two is good enough for me until the later miles. Take your gels roughly every hour. They are packed with carbohydrates and caffeine to help keep you energized.

4. No new gear on race day.

This is a classic rule. You don't want to change anything on the day of the marathon. You might think that a new set of shoes will serve you well, but they won't—not even the exact same brand and model. Get your marathon shoes a month or so before the race so that you have plenty of time to log some miles and break them in. The same thing goes for the less important stuff like shorts, shirts, and socks. You want to be familiar with the fabric. Severe unexpected chafing is an easy way to ruin a race.

5. No new foods on race weekend.

Stick with what you know you can digest easily. Prerace meals are not the time to head out for exotic spicy Indian or sushi. Your standard reasonable pasta dish will serve you well. The same thing goes for during the race. Pack your own sports gels or train with the brand you know the race will serve (the race Web site should supply this information) to give your digestive tract some time to get used to it.

6. Get some technical material gear.

This might seem like a no-brainer, but I did the majority of my early races in cotton T-shirts simply because I didn't know any better. Tech fabrics wick away sweat and are super lightweight. They also have a certain "breathability" factor that other materials simply don't have.

7. Don't forget to warm up.

Thirty minutes before the race, trot around for five or ten minutes to loosen up your legs. It might seem counterproductive, but your quads and calves will thank you later. Don't do anything strenuous, just jog out the sleepiness.

8. Find your pacing group and stick with them.

This one isn't for everyone, but if you could use the camaraderie, find your pacing bunny (they will be in the corral lined up according to their speeds) and stick with the group. Many marathons will have pacers all the way up to five hours and thirty minutes or six hours, and they provide some great motivation and conversation to help keep your mind off the miles.

9. Leave the iPod at home during the race.

Come on, it's the freaking marathon. There will be thousands of spectators screaming, bands shredding, and homeless dudes yelling. Keep the earbuds out and take it all in. Plus, many marathons urge you not to wear them or straight-up ban them for safety reasons.

Addendum: Get your name on your bib or write it on. The spectators screaming your name will boost your morale when you need it most.

10. When you finish your race, you have forty-eight guilt-free hours to show it off.

Less than one percent of the world's population (and as low as .1 percent, according to some studies) has finished a marathon. Celebrate accordingly. You and your bad self deserve the finest that Chili's has to offer. And feel free to wear your medal through it all. You earned it.

Honorable mentions:

Thank the volunteers. These races don't happen without volunteers. The least you can do is let them know that you appreciate their help. I also hear they really like custom-made songs.

Smile for the cameras. Most marathons have a pro photo company there to snap action shots of racers throughout the course. They'll most likely be kneeling, wearing a backward cap, holding one of those cameras with the long lens. Smile at them and give them a thumbs-up. It's hard to look good while running, but a smile goes a long way.

After I had been running for two or three months, my good friend Charlie got inspired to run a mile nonstop for

the first time in a couple of years. He confidently strapped on some running shoes and we went out into the night to time his mile. Now, Charlie is a big dude, but he's also a proud dude, and his confidence manifested itself in one of the best lessons for new runners.

He crouched down as I got the stopwatch ready. I counted it down for him to make it feel as official as possible. "Three . . . Two . . . One . . . Go!" And with that, Charlie took off at a dead sprint. You would have thought he was timing his hundred-meter time. I swear there were sparks coming from beneath his feet. It took me a couple of seconds to recover from the initial wave of laughter, but I slowly began my jog to catch up with him, knowing that his pace was completely unsustainable and would probably prevent him from finishing at all.

"I messed up," he huffed at me after a quarter of a mile. "I started too fast."

This is one of the most avoidable mistakes for a new runner and even a first-time marathoner. But it's easy to understand why it happens. Once that gun blasts to start the marathon, your nerves and adrenaline can go into full-on freak-out mode. You're surrounded by thousands and thousands of runners, and your natural instinct is to bolt. It's so important to resist this temptation. Running too quickly, even for one or two miles, can come back to absolutely destroy you toward the end of the race. Stay in your zone; don't worry about anyone else. In fact, it's smart to aim for ten to fifteen seconds slower per mile than your goal marathon pace and force yourself to stick to it. After two miles or so, when the field begins to thin a bit, push up to your goal pace and reap the rewards of feeling fresh when you reach miles twenty to twenty-six. You'll be smiling your way to the finish line as the people who didn't stick to their plan are crumpled over on the curb.

I almost made the same mistake as Charlie at the Denver marathon. Jed, Pa, and I were dropped off two blocks from the starting line, and we immediately felt an excitement in the air. By the time we made it to the starting line, about 150 yards deep, the buzz had grown. As far as I could see, in front of me and behind, there were runners. It was an amazing thing to see. I looked at Pa. "This is really cool," I said.

"It is," he replied as he stared ahead. I could tell he was excited. I was excited. Everyone was excited. In fact, by the time the gun blasted ten minutes later, all three of us were a little too excited.

"Dude, we have to slow down," Jed said after looking at his watch. "We're averaging nine-minute miles."

"Let's just do it," I said, jokingly. "We can keep it up."

Thankfully, Pa checked my ego and helped prevent me from burning out. "You go ahead," Pa replied. "We'll see you in five miles."

This is another way that my dad saved me and got me on the right track. He and Jed always knew how to keep my ego in check. Before long, we found our groove and were knocking out ten-and-a-half-minute miles left and right. The first hour went by quickly. We didn't talk much, as we were satisfied to just take in the experience. When I made the turn at the half-marathon mark, I remember thinking about how good I felt, and that it wasn't going to be as hard to finish as I had imagined. By this time, I was running alone. Jed was consistently thirty meters ahead of me and Pa was thirty meters in front of him. Jed needed the padding, though, because he had to stop to pee every seven or eight miles, something Pa and I were always making fun of him about.

Time was flying by. I felt good. My legs were loose, my lungs were pumping, and I couldn't even find my heartbeat with my hand. The ground below me was a blur.

do life

We approached an unofficial aid station at mile seventeen. "What's this?" Jed asked me.

"How am I supposed to know?" I answered.

We got to the table quickly. The lady on duty held out some pretzels. We both grabbed a handful as we ran past. I ate four of them and regretted it immediately. The salt and crumbs caked my mouth and throat. I tossed the remaining ten or so on the ground and heard them crunching under the feet of the runners behind me.

I looked ahead at Jed, who had done the same thing. He and Pa were running next to each other. I still felt good. My mouth was a little dry, but it wasn't anything that a little water at nineteen wouldn't cure. And that's when it hit me. I couldn't breathe. Well, I could, but I had lost my breath. My lungs were heaving in and out at an awkward rhythm, and my pace had slowed to a jog to compensate. I was scared, but when I heard Jed tell Pa that he couldn't breathe, I took comfort in the fact that it wasn't just me.

The miles were no longer flying by. Every step felt forced. Pain seared through my legs. My shins were twigs waiting to be snapped. My left big toe hurt, my right big toe hurt, and my pinkie toes hurt, as well. I began to live for the Gatorade. Every time a mile sign appeared, I rejoiced—not because it was another mile down, but because I knew there would be volunteers handing out lemon-lime goodness in roughly two hundred meters. At mile nineteen, I began taking two cups of Gatorade and two cups of water. I would drink the Gatorades and pour the water on my head. It was a ritual I perfected at our first half marathon and never forgot. But this day, the aid station at mile nineteen would be the last one I remembered with clarity. That's when I hit the wall. The wall is simply when a marathon runner's body just, for lack of a better term, gives out. It usually happens somewhere between miles eighteen and twenty-two. The result is physical torment, but it's even worse for the mind, because you begin to doubt yourself. Water won't help, because it is more of a psychological problem.

This is when mental techniques become crucial in order to get you to the end. Remind yourself that your mind is playing tricks on you. Your body is capable of finishing; you just have to get your mind on the same track. It's easier said than done, but try different coping techniques until you find the one that works. Talk out loud to yourself. Dedicate the next mile to someone you love and let the thought of them motivate you to keep going.

Some runners use a meditative process or a mantra to help them overcome the wall. If you let go and try to empty your mind of worries, the right thoughts and rituals will come to you. Over time, I've come up with a thought process that keeps me going even in the worst moments. I simply tell myself, "No matter how tough it is now, the next three hours are going to happen whether you quit or not. You might as well grit your teeth, deal with the pain, and finish." Barring an actual injury, it helps get me through anything knowing that no matter what, in five hours I'm not going to be on the course anymore, so I might as well get that medal.

Unless it's absolutely mandatory or you're risking injury, don't sit down or stop for any extended period of time. Whenever they get the chance to rest, your leg muscles are going to seize up something fierce. Slow down to a jog or walk, but don't stop completely. The same techniques, of course, can apply to every part of your life. When things get tough, simply remind yourself that this (no matter what "this" is) will end. Pain is finite. Suffering is finite. You will get through this if you just keep going. The wall doesn't stick

around forever, but it is easier to defeat with a partner or group, so reach out to your running buddy if you have one.

The main thing is to keep trucking. You're not going to get through by staying in one place. Take it slowly and remember how far you've come. Compare the hundreds of miles you've trekked to get to this point to the few measly miles that you have left. Remember how strong your legs are, how sturdy your feet are. Think about how good that medal is going to feel around your neck or how cool that 26.2 sticker is going to look on your bumper. Think about the people who have supported you and believed in you— the people who are there at the finish line cheering for you. Those are the things that are going to get you through to that line.

When I hit the wall in Denver, it was Jed and Pa who got me through, just like they had gotten me out of my rut and motivated me to finish the half marathon only a few months before. We threw our hands in the air as we crossed the finish line and I immediately stopped. I put my hands on my knees and stared at the ground. It was a heavy moment. I was physically exhausted in a way that I've never felt before, but the rush of adrenaline that came with it was equally powerful and unique. I looked around at the thousands of smiling faces and felt an enormous wave of relief. We were done.

For a moment, I thought about how far I had come. In only ten months, I had gone from weighing 365 pounds to running a 5K, from running a 5K to finishing a 10K, from running a half marathon now to 26.2. I had tested myself and I had passed. I found Pa and hugged him. "I couldn't have finished it without you," I said, and I meant it.

"That's why we're here," he said.

To say I fulfilled a lifelong dream that day would be a lie. In fact, it would be an understatement. Instead, I did something that I had previously perceived to be so far from possible that I hadn't even dared to dream it.

We celebrated, as usual, with a victory meal. We told jokes, we laughed, and we admired each other's medals. We had done it. I felt like I was sitting on the pinnacle of the fitness world, completely content with my ribs, fries, and soda, when Jed uttered the words that would change our lives forever.

"So . . . ," he started. "What do you guys think about an Ironman?"

▶ READER QUESTION

"I realized that I needed to change my life about six months ago, but I still haven't found the motivation to actually do anything about it. What advice do you have for me?"

Think about the past six months and how quickly they've gone by. Think about how you would feel right now if you had made the decision back then to buckle down, train hard, eat right, and do all the things that go into healthy living. Think about how much progress you would have made. The next six months are going to pass just as quickly. How do you want to feel six months from now? Do you want to be filled with regret over still doing nothing to make your life better, or do you want to be living a better, healthier, happier life? Why not start now and give your future self the gratification and satisfaction of having done the work?

Six months goes by in the blink of an eye; you might as well buckle down and reward yourself. So start today. The same thing goes for when you hit a wall or a rut, or find yourself on a plateau. Think about yourself looking back a few months down the road and how much

TESTING YOURSELF

happier you'll be if you push hard and give yourself that happy ending. Start now. Your life is waiting for you.

───────── Reader Testimonial ─────────

My identical twin sister and I have lost eighty pounds each and are on our way to losing a hundred pounds! We started running. As we lost weight, a 5K was our first goal two years ago. Since then, we have completed several 5Ks and 10Ks, a triathlon, and two half marathons. This year, it will be a full marathon. Every step of the way, we have lost weight together, crossed finish lines together, and we were even on national TV together trying to motivate people. We started a blog recently and will continue to pay it forward as we continue on our journey. —Jessica M

MARATHON TRAINING GUIDE

This is a beginner's marathon training guide, so we're going to stay away from hill workouts and focus on getting the miles under our belts. If you want to push yourself a little farther, every two weeks swap out a midweek run for a nice thirty-minute or hour-long hill workout.

WEEK ONE

DAY ONE: 3 easy miles

DAY TWO: cross 30 minutes

DAY THREE: 4 easy miles

DAY FOUR: 3 tempo miles

DAY FIVE: rest

DAY SIX: 6 easy miles

DAY SEVEN: 2 easy miles

WEEK ONE TOTAL: 18 miles

WEEK TWO

DAY ONE: 3 easy miles

DAY TWO: cross 30 minutes

DAY THREE: 4 moderate miles

DAY FOUR: 4 tempo miles

DAY FIVE: rest

marathon training guide

DAY SIX: 7 easy miles

DAY SEVEN: 2 easy miles

WEEK TWO TOTAL: 20 miles

WEEK THREE

DAY ONE: 3 moderate miles

DAY TWO: cross 30 minutes

DAY THREE: 4 moderate miles

DAY FOUR: 5 tempo miles

DAY FIVE: rest

DAY SIX: 8 easy miles

DAY SEVEN: 2 easy miles

WEEK THREE TOTAL: 22 miles

WEEK FOUR

DAY ONE: 3 moderate miles

DAY TWO: cross 30 minutes

DAY THREE: 5 moderate miles

DAY FOUR: 6 tempo miles

DAY FIVE: rest

DAY SIX: 9 easy miles

DAY SEVEN: 2 easy miles

WEEK FOUR TOTAL: 25 miles

WEEK FIVE

DAY ONE: 4 moderate miles

DAY TWO: cross 30 minutes

DAY THREE: 5 moderate miles

DAY FOUR: 5 tempo miles

DAY FIVE: rest

DAY SIX: 10 easy miles

DAY SEVEN: 2 easy miles

WEEK FIVE TOTAL: 26 miles

WEEK SIX

DAY ONE: 4 moderate miles

DAY TWO: cross 45 minutes

DAY THREE: 5 moderate miles

DAY FOUR: 6 tempo miles

DAY FIVE: rest

DAY SIX: 12 easy miles

DAY SEVEN: 2 easy miles

WEEK SIX TOTAL: 29 miles

WEEK SEVEN

DAY ONE: 4 moderate miles

DAY TWO: cross 45 minutes

marathon training guide

DAY THREE: 4 moderate miles

DAY FOUR: 6 tempo miles

DAY FIVE: rest

DAY SIX: 13.1 easy miles

DAY SEVEN: 2 easy miles

WEEK SEVEN TOTAL: 29.1 miles

WEEK EIGHT

DAY ONE: 4 moderate miles

DAY TWO: cross 45 minutes

DAY THREE: 6 moderate miles

DAY FOUR: 6 tempo miles

DAY FIVE: rest

DAY SIX: 14 easy miles

DAY SEVEN: 2 easy miles

WEEK EIGHT TOTAL: 32 miles

WEEK NINE

DAY ONE: 4 moderate miles

DAY TWO: cross 45 minutes

DAY THREE: 5 moderate miles

DAY FOUR: 7 tempo miles

DAY FIVE: rest

DAY SIX: 15 easy miles

DAY SEVEN: 2 easy miles

WEEK NINE TOTAL: 33 miles

WEEK TEN

DAY ONE: 4 moderate miles

DAY TWO: cross 45 minutes

DAY THREE: 6 moderate miles

DAY FOUR: 8 tempo miles

DAY FIVE: rest

DAY SIX: 12 easy miles

DAY SEVEN: 3 easy miles

WEEK TEN TOTAL: 33 miles

WEEK ELEVEN

DAY ONE: 4 moderate miles

DAY TWO: cross 45 minutes

DAY THREE: 6 moderate miles

DAY FOUR: 8 tempo miles

DAY FIVE: rest

DAY SIX: 16 easy miles

DAY SEVEN: 3 easy miles

WEEK ELEVEN TOTAL: 37 miles

marathon training guide

WEEK TWELVE

DAY ONE: 4 moderate miles

DAY TWO: cross 45 minutes

DAY THREE: 5 moderate miles

DAY FOUR: 7 tempo miles

DAY FIVE: rest

DAY SIX: 18 easy miles

DAY SEVEN: 3 easy miles

WEEK TWELVE TOTAL: 37 miles

WEEK THIRTEEN

DAY ONE: 5 moderate miles

DAY TWO: cross 45 minutes

DAY THREE: 6 moderate miles

DAY FOUR: 8 tempo miles

DAY FIVE: rest

DAY SIX: 13 easy miles

DAY SEVEN: 3 easy miles

WEEK THIRTEEN TOTAL: 35 miles

WEEK FOURTEEN

DAY ONE: 5 moderate miles

DAY TWO: cross 45 minutes

DAY THREE: 6 moderate miles

DAY FOUR: 7 tempo miles

DAY FIVE: rest

DAY SIX: 19–20 easy miles

DAY SEVEN: 2 easy miles

WEEK FOURTEEN TOTAL: 39–40 miles

WEEK FIFTEEN (taper begins)

DAY ONE: 4 moderate miles

DAY TWO: cross 45 minutes

DAY THREE: 3 moderate miles

DAY FOUR: 4 moderate miles

DAY FIVE: rest

DAY SIX: 10 easy miles

DAY SEVEN: 2 easy miles

WEEK FIFTEEN TOTAL: 23 miles

WEEK SIXTEEN

DAY ONE: 3 easy miles

DAY TWO: 2 easy miles

DAY THREE: rest

DAY FOUR: rest

DAY FIVE: rest

marathon training guide

DAY SIX: walk/jog 20 minutes

DAY SEVEN: MARATHON

WEEK SIXTEEN TOTAL: 31.2 miles

8

pushing
yourself to
the limit

IF YOU TEST yourself and you pass that test, if you reach goal after goal after goal, your new goal must become never to allow yourself to become complacent. In our lives, in our relationships, in our jobs, and in running, we must fight a constant battle against complacency by going farther, going faster, and never slowing down. Jed, Pa, and I signed up for Ironman Louisville in January of 2010, exactly one year after I started at 365 pounds and couldn't even jog a mile. I was proud of myself, but I wouldn't let that pride turn into ego—not this time. I was determined to keep on going to find out exactly what I was capable of.

We filled out our registrations and each paid six hundred dollars to get in. We were scared, but we were also committed. We weren't "ready" to do an Ironman, but we couldn't wait until we were ready and risk becoming smug in the meantime. In life, you have to commit yourself to new challenges when you're almost ready for them, not when you're so ready that they're not even exciting anymore. Commit yourself and *then* do the work necessary to prepare. If we all waited until we were completely ready to get married, would anyone ever do it? If people waited until they were a hundred percent ready to have kids, would the world's population dry up? The stars are never going to align perfectly for your new adventure. You're never going to have the perfect schedule or enough money in your savings account. You have to pave your way through the adversity and make the perfect situation for yourself, because waiting for it to be safe and perfect is completely beside the point.

When you become a more experienced runner and have been through a few trials on the road, you need to stop and ask yourself what's in it for you. What keeps you going? I once asked my dad why he runs, why he signs up for races, why he pays good money to put himself through figurative hell, both in the adventure races that he did with Jed and the races we've all done together.

"Part of it is the cool factor," he told me. "Over the course of the past few years, I've had the opportunity to do some things that many people haven't. I have waded up to my neck in alligator-infested Florida ponds at midnight, rappelled off a two-hundred-foot water tower, been hypothermic in several whitewater rivers in midwinter, gotten caught in a near flash flood during a two a.m. thunderstorm in the Texas desert, and wound up in a dazed heap many times after sailing over the handlebars of my mountain bike. It just doesn't get any better than that."

Many long-distance runners are like Pa. They like the idea of being the guy (or girl) who does crazy stuff, the one who pushes himself further than everyone else. It's a powerful feeling. There is a certain satisfaction that comes along with replying, "Twenty-mile run on Saturday and fifty-mile bike ride on Sunday," when someone casually asks about your weekend. It's different and it's cool. It's cool to drive halfway across the country, wake up at three in the morning, put some Band-Aids over your nipples, throw on some clothes, and swim, bike, and run farther than most people can possibly dream of going. It's even cooler to get slightly injured during the ordeal—nothing major, just a little blood, a sprain or two, some minor frostbite, or a pronounced limp that doesn't go away for at least several days. These badges of honor separate us from the rest of the video-game-playing, TV-watching, gas-guzzling, fast-food-eating masses. This is exactly how I distinguish myself from the person I used to be.

So, I'll ask you this—what sets you apart?

The moment I crossed the finish line at the Denver Marathon, I became part of a minuscule percentage of the earth's population. The part of the census that wakes up each morning and doesn't take no for an answer. The part that sees 26.2 miles not as an arbitrary distance, but as a challenge issued from the universe. The part that answers that challenge by saying, "Come and get it."

One of the best things about this notion of the cool factor is that we get to decide for ourselves how cool we want to be—we set our own bar. Most of us are not going to swim from Cuba to Miami, run across America in fifty days, or do an Antarctic marathon. We have to realize that there's always going to be someone doing something that's more amazing, more dangerous, or more physically challenging or death-defying than anything that we will personally be tempted to do. But all of us can challenge ourselves to do the next cool thing, to push ourselves to our own personal limits.

PUSHING YOURSELF TO THE LIMIT

advice for running in cold weather

THE NUMBER-ONE QUESTION I get from new runners as we approach the chilly winter months is what to expect from cold-weather running. There are definitely some differences between hot- and cold-weather running to be aware of, but running in the cold certainly isn't as awful as most new runners fear. I hope that these tips will help you feel confident in tackling that first icy run, and many more to follow.

1. Expect faster times

Most runners agree that they go faster in the cold weather than they do when it's hot, and many runners also feel that they can go greater distances in the cold. The reason for this is that your body doesn't lose electrolytes as quickly in the cold, and so your muscles can warm up more slowly over the course of your run.

2. Don't overdress

I ran my first 5K in January. That morning, the thermometer said twenty-two degrees with a windchill of nineteen. Having never run in temperatures anywhere near that (I trained on an indoor track), I headed out wearing all the winter gear I could find—full-length thermal underwear, wind pants, sweater, face mask, beanie, and scarf. This was a huge mistake. By mile one, I was so hot that I began shedding clothes with no concern about whether or not I'd ever get them back.

Now I know better. For temperatures down to forty-five degrees, I wear shorts with a short-sleeve tech shirt. For temps between forty-five and thirty-two degrees, I wear shorts and a long-sleeve tech shirt. Anything below freezing calls for long thermals, shorts, a tech T-shirt, and a running jacket with gloves. Leave the big puffy coat at home. Lower body layers like leggings and tights aren't as suffocating, so feel free to experiment, but err on the side of minimalist up top.

3. Lung burn eventually goes away

I can't tell you how many times I tried to start running during the winter months and quickly became discouraged because of that awful burning sensation when I breathed. What most beginning runners don't realize is that this doesn't last. It actually only takes a few runs to get your lungs used to the frosty air, and then the rest of your winter runs will be pain-free.

4. Gear is your best friend

Running fashionistas, rejoice! Winter is when we finally get our best fashion choices. From black running gloves to trendy headbands, earmuffs, and beanies, winter running gear will help you feel professional while motivating you to head out there for a winter run.

5. Hydration is still important

While you don't lose as many fluids to sweat in the winter as you do in summer, you still need to make sure that you stay hydrated when running in the cold. Try room-temperature water rather than ice-cold stuff, or just eat some snow as you run (unless dogs are frequently walked along your route).

For me and Jed and Pa, our next cool thing was Ironman. It started as a pipe dream and quickly became an impending, daunting adventure, but a reality nonetheless—and

that was cool. We were scared, but we were psyched. And we were a team.

We did our first hundred-mile training ride together. I was on my bike—a thin black road bike with one-inch-wide tires like you see in the Tour de France—hurtling down a hill in central Arkansas at forty-seven miles per hour. Jed was twenty feet behind me and Pa another twenty feet behind him. There wasn't a single cloud in the sky to block the merciless sun. Forty-seven miles per hour. In a car, that's nothing. On a bike, though? It's both unnerving and exhilarating to go that fast with nothing more than a fifteen-pound frame of aluminum standing between you and the unforgiving asphalt.

We were careening down this hill to gain as much momentum as possible to take us up the next hill, which was even bigger. We needed all the help we could get. Biking uphill is a beast, surprisingly harder than running. We were just near the bottom of the first hill when out of the corner of my eye I saw a dog run out from the forest next to the highway. He was headed right for me.

"Dog!" I yelled.

When you're on a road bike going downhill, there's really no room for sudden swerves. So this was it, I figured. I was about to die. And then I realized that it was even worse than I thought. It wasn't a dog at all. It was a cow. Behind me, I heard my dad scream, *"Fucking cow! Ahhh!"*

Just as the cow was about to run into my bike, she lost her footing on the grass next to the pavement and fell face-first into the mud. Her head landed eighteen inches from my tire. I had averted disaster. I took a breath. But, somehow, the cow regained his footing, picked herself up, and headed straight for Jed, who yelled an obscenity but had enough time to swerve to the left, narrowly missing her. That left

Pa, who still hadn't stopped screaming. Pa shifted to the right and dodged the cow, coming close enough to touch her tail. The cow let out a booming "*Moo*" and kept running.

We stopped our bikes and lay on the ground, realizing how narrowly we'd all escaped death. After a few moments of scared silence, we began laughing. We were twenty miles into our scheduled 112-mile training ride, already had first-degree sunburns, were hot and tired, and had almost been killed by a cow.

My dad and brother are now my two best friends. The team we've formed through running and racing has been my catalyst through life over the past few years. I know that many families don't share a bond nearly as strong as the one we share today. But as I've said, it wasn't always like this for us, either. We were mere feet away from one another for most of my life, and we might as well have been on different planets. Today, we live thousands of miles apart and it's like we're all roommates. We do life together and everything has changed.

My relationship with my mom has always been good, but she is prouder of me now than she's ever been, and that has only helped make things even better between us. She often e-mails me to tell me how proud she is of me, and she recently drove six hours to see me make the keynote speech at the Lincoln Marathon. Doing life out in the open gives those around you an opportunity to get closer.

This only illustrates how drastically all your relationships will change once you get out of the negative, addictive cycles that may be holding you back and start doing life. The key is honesty. When you're no longer living in denial and can finally be honest with yourself about who you are, what you want out of life, and what you're going to do in order to get it, you become a little more honest with everyone

PUSHING YOURSELF TO THE LIMIT

else around you. This improves the quality of your relationships because it allows others to help you. It allows you to let them in.

When I was obese and sad and lonely, I kept everyone at arm's length because I was ashamed of myself. I would always tell people that I was fine, that all was well, when it really wasn't fine at all. Our natural instinct as humans is to hide our struggles by keeping them to ourselves, because we're afraid of ridicule or humiliation. We're afraid of what people might think of us if we open up to them. But I've found that so much of this is all in our heads.

Far more often than not, when you open up to someone, they aren't going to laugh. Instead, they're going to be there for you. They're going to welcome you with open arms and either do what they can to help with your journey or take an active role and join you. Be open; be public with your goals. You never know who you'll connect with and how the relationships in your own life will change as a result.

what exactly is an ironman?

IF YOU'VE EVER been driving around and seen a mysterious bumper sticker that says, simply, "140.6," you were looking at the bumper of a proud Ironman finisher. Ironman is a beast, and the finishers wear the bumper stickers like a badge of honor.

Ironman is a 140.6-mile-long triathlon. It's when you wake up at four a.m., eat a quick breakfast, put on some clothes, and then jump into a large body of water. Upon entering the water, you swim 2.4 miles with three thousand other athletes kicking and slapping about like crazed cats who were dropped into a pool. You swim for what feels like an eternity; you swim until it's all you know.

When you finally get out of the water, you feel like you weigh a thousand pounds. You change your clothes, eat a banana, throw on some sunblock, and jump on a bike. You then ride that bike for 112 miles. Have you ever sat on a two-inch-wide bike seat for seven hours? It's not the most pleasant thing. Then you get off the bike, throw on your running shoes, and run 26.2 miles—a full marathon. Your body betrays you, your mind crumbles, but you keep going.

The best in the world finish the Ironman in eight or so hours, and the final finishers come in right around midnight. In Ironman, there is a strict seventeen-hour cutoff. No one is allowed to even come across the line after the time is up. It's brutal, but that's how it goes. I strongly believe that anyone can do an Ironman if he or she puts in the time to train. It is indeed a lot of training (fifteen to twenty-two hours per week for four to six months), but the payoff—being an Ironman—is worth every bit of it.

At this point, I was down to my goal weight of 218 pounds, but my focus had shifted from frantically trying to lose weight to trying to become the fittest and happiest person I could be. As my ultimate goal changed from a number on the scale to a state of mind, something else clicked in place for me. Losing weight and exercising are simple, I realized. They are just things that you do. But you have to find something bigger on which to focus your efforts—something outside yourself. I had found racing and competing. It kept me focused on a new goal, and that was happiness.

Soon enough, we were there, signing in, weighing in, and checking in. We got our Ironman bracelets, and it was official—we were going to attempt something that not long ago would have seemed impossible, had I even known what it was. It was fifteen months before that Jed and I stood on the shore of Beaverfork Lake, about to compete in our first triathlon. The announcer came over the loudspeaker and said that there were a few athletes competing in the triathlon that had also done a half Ironman the day before. We applauded politely as I turned to Jed curiously.

"What are the distances for a half Ironman?"

"One-point-two mile swim, fifty-six-mile bike, and a half-marathon run," he replied.

I was stunned.

"So . . . a full Ironman would be, like . . . two-point-four, one hundred twelve, and then a full marathon?"

"Yep."

"No, thank you," I replied.

He laughed, and then we jumped in.

Fifteen months later, we were standing in line with three thousand other athletes, waiting to jump in yet again, but this time into something much bigger and scarier.

Two-point-four, one hundred and twelve, and twenty-six-point-two.

The gates opened up at around six a.m., letting the athletes enter the dock area. Soon after, a bugler played the National Anthem and Kentucky's state song, and then the pro athletes (who start ten minutes early) jumped in. After we watched the pros slash through the water at jaw-dropping speeds, our own cannon blasted and we began our first Ironman.

The swim section of a triathlon, particularly one with thousands of participants, doesn't exactly lend itself to introspective moments of reflection. It's like swimming through a washing machine. Everywhere you turn, there are legs and arms slapping and swinging in every direction. You have to constantly guard against getting kicked in the goggles or slapped in the head, which doesn't allow much time to analyze or think about what you're doing. This mind-set of simple self-defense started the day out perfectly for me. I told myself not to think. All I had to do was stay afloat.

We made our turnaround after about thirteen hundred meters, and swam downstream with the current. It was cool to look at a nice view of downtown Louisville after spending the first third of the swim in a dam between land and an island. Eventually, I could see the exit, but I continued focusing my efforts on not getting excited or pushing too hard.

As I made my way to the dock, I glanced at my watch: one hour, forty minutes. This was a new 2.4-mile record for me, and I hadn't overexerted in the least. This gave me a huge boost of confidence. I was slightly dizzy as I made my way through the enormous, screaming crowd, but this is normal while trying to walk after being in the water for a hundred minutes. I made my way to the transition area, forcing myself to walk rather than run with the rest of the athletes. Even though I didn't run, I was encouraged by how great I felt. I ducked into the tent and grabbed my gear bag from a volunteer.

With the bonus five to ten minutes that I had accumulated on the swim section, I decided to take it easy and rest in the changing tent to cool down. The volunteers were really incredible about getting me everything I needed, and this was a really nice way to chill out between sections. After putting on all my clothes, turning on all my GPS devices, and making sure I didn't forget anything, I got slathered up in sunscreen by a volunteer and made my way to the bike. I fought the urge to steal one of the thousands of tri bikes there that cost more than my car, but eventually found my way to my used five-hundred-dollar road bike with standard pedals and no aero bars. I reminded myself it's not about the ride; it's about the rider, and I hopped on.

PUSHING YOURSELF TO THE LIMIT

While I was making my way to the transition exit, Sarah Catherine, Jed's wife, yelled at me to let me know Jed was only three minutes behind me.

"Really!" I yelled back, thinking I had misheard or that she was confused.

"Yeah!" she yelled.

In all the 2.4-mile swims that Jed and I had done that summer, he had never finished in less than two hours. The fact that he'd somehow notched a 1:43 meant that he had either thrown pacing out the window or caught some luck with a huge current. I reminded myself to focus on my own race and headed out on the bike.

The first ten miles of the bike course were flat, but then it got heinous. I forced myself to stay at 15.5 to sixteen miles per hour and never let my heart rate get above 150. "Just spin," I kept saying to myself. "Don't push." The number of bikers passing me (including Jed at mile five) was a little disheartening, but all the prerace advice I had read told me that I would be passing all these people at mile eighty after their legs had given out from pushing too hard too early.

Pa caught up with me at the fifteen-mile aid station and we rode together for pretty much the entire race, even managing to hold conversations when we could. Although it was good to have a riding buddy, our conversations were sparse because of the insane number of hills the bike course had to offer. We knew it would be filled with rolling hills, but we didn't expect it to be constant up and down. All we could do was observe and react, spin efficiently uphill, and enjoy the speed of the downhill. We did it, and it worked.

The bike section of Ironman Louisville includes a thirty-mile loop that circles through La Grange, a town that holds a spectator festival. Sarah Catherine and my girlfriend at the time had set up shop there, so we got to see them twice, at miles thirty-eight and sixty-eight, which was great. We managed to catch up with Jed around mile fifty and assess how everything was going. He was struggling a bit, but he was confident that he would be able to finish. We made our way through La Grange a second time, passing the girls again, this time as a team. They gave us a loud cheer and we continued on.

After the second pass through, I was a little skeptical about Jed's confidence in finishing. His pace slowed dramatically, his eyes looked very weary, and I began to worry. Without realizing it, Pa and I would get so far ahead that we would stop to make sure he was okay. At mile eighty, he told us that he was sure he could complete the bike if he could just get through the next fifteen miles to the downhill and flat sections of the course. It was heartbreaking to see him struggle so much, particularly because I knew that it could just as easily have been me. We all have good days and bad ones. I was getting lucky with a good day. The final thirty miles were as perfect as they could have been for me, and I entered the bike dismount area with extreme confidence, both mentally and physically.

I sat back down in the changing tent and switched into my running gear. Pa came in after about ten minutes. We recapped the ride and relaxed while waiting on Jed. The minutes ticked by slowly, but we had again beaten our expectations, so we could afford to spend the time. Finally, Jed came through the entrance, but he didn't look good.

"We have to help him," I told Pa. He agreed.

"Jed, sit down. Tell us what you need," I said.

He relaxed and cooled down while we helped him with drinks and electrolyte tablets for his cramps.

"Take it easy," I told him. "We have all day." I was nervously glancing at my watch, though, knowing anything

could go wrong in the 26.2-mile trek that lay ahead of us. He gained his composure and we headed to the marathon starting point with seven hours and forty minutes to get through. It was obvious that our run/walk strategy was going to be demoted to a walk-most-of-the-time-and-jog-when-you-feel-like-it situation in order to help Jed. In the moment, it was slightly frustrating because I felt as good as I could have hoped and wanted very badly to run. But this was something we were doing as a team, something we were going to finish together. It didn't really matter if the time said 16:59 or 14:00, as long as we finished together.

The run course started with a two-mile, one-time-only out-and-back across the river, before settling into a twelve-mile, out-and-back that you do twice. After four miles of our walk/jog, I realized that I needed to take advantage of how good I felt and put some bonus minutes in the bank in case things got bad in the late miles and I had to slow down dramatically. Pa shared my sentiment, and after talking to Jed to make sure he was okay to do it alone, we pushed ahead at a nice twelve-minute-per-mile pace. The good thing about the out-and-back nature of the course was that we could meet up with Jed every six miles on the turnaround to assess everything. Each time, he told us that he was hurting, but that he thought he could make it.

Our half-marathon split was three hours and three minutes, a lot better than we had anticipated during our training, so we began to feel a little more confident. It was mile fourteen, though, that brought the pick-me-up that we needed. The Louisville running course infamously takes runners who are halfway done within two hundred yards of the finish line before starting the second loop. You get close enough to see everything and hear the screams. Most of the course previews I had read expressed frustration with this because it is a severe tease, but seeing the finish line and the huge raucous crowd of spectators and supporters there bought tears to my eyes, because it was the first time it had hit me that we were actually going to finish. We had only twelve more miles to go.

The hours crept by and the sun made its way down. Our bodies hurt, but the blisters on our feet and the soreness deep in our legs were trumped by the satisfaction of each passing mile marker and every spectator who yelled out encouragement. Each pat on the back from a friendly volunteer relieved the pain that seared through our ankles. The backaches were nothing compared to the inspiration that hit when the seventy-three-year-old man we were running next to grimaced in pain with each torturous step, but continued on with unbelievable resolve.

Mile twenty-two . . . mile twenty-three . . . mile twenty-four . . .

By this time, most of the casual supporters in the neighborhood and in their yards had gone to bed. The aid stations were understocked and only held four or five people to man them. We knew what lay ahead, though: a finish line full of our friends and family along with thousands of crazy spectators waiting to cheer us on. We made it to mile twenty-five and nailed down our plan. We would get to the final aid station and wait on Jed, who was now about 1.5 miles behind the two of us.

When we arrived, the volunteers encouraged us and asked us why we were stopping when we were so close. We explained the situation and they let us know that they were there to help if we needed anything. We thanked them and began the wait, at which point I looked down and remembered that I was wearing white, a very unfortunate color for a big guy in finish line photos.

PUSHING YOURSELF TO THE LIMIT

"Dude, switch me shirts," I said. Pa was wearing a nice, slimming black shirt.

"What? Why?" he replied.

"I look terrible in this thing. I only wore it so I wouldn't get too hot."

"I've always hated you," he asserted as he pulled off his shirt.

We exchanged them, and that's when the dizziness and nausea hit me. If I kept standing still, I would pass out and have to drop out of the race a mile from the finish.

"We have to go. I'm about to faint. We can still wait for Jed, but I have to keep moving." We walked up the next few blocks to the last turn before the finish line and continued to wait on Jed. Eleven twenty-five turned to eleven thirty and then eleven forty. There were only twenty minutes until the cutoff time, and Ironman cutoffs are no joke. They shut down at midnight with no exceptions. The nervousness built and we started talking about what we would do if he didn't make it. How long would we wait?

We kept our gaze fixed onto the corner where he would make his turn—that's if he had been able to make it.

"Is that him?" Pa asked.

"No," I answered, regretfully. Pa has notoriously bad eyes.

Eleven forty-five . . .

Eleven forty-six . . .

Eleven forty-seven . . .

And then, there he was. His walk had deteriorated to a zombielike shuffle, but there he was. I've never been so happy to see him before or since. We rushed to meet him and make sure that he was okay. Seeing him walk through pain that I couldn't even imagine brought me to tears for the second time that day, and then our excitement began to rise. A group of spectators on the sidewalk yelled encouragingly as we made our turn onto Fourth Street. The finish line in all its glory was only five hundred yards away.

"Let's jog it in!" Jed yelled.

I was shocked, but we happily obliged. Pa was in the middle, I was to his left, and Jed was on his right. The chute was completely empty for us to make our finish. Each step felt like it was happening in slow motion. The crowd roared, children held out their hands for high fives, and athletes who had finished hours before us lined the streets to cheer us on.

Mike Reilly, the voice of Ironman, brought us home. We approached the line and he yelled out the words we'd been training for six months to hear. "Here is a family of three! John Davis and his two sons!" And then, "*John, Jed, Ben! You! Are! Ironmen!*"

We crossed the lines with our hands in the air and immediately found each other for the most meaningful hug of my life. Volunteers hung medals on our necks and it was official. We had done it.

Jed found the closest chair, and Pa sat next to him to make sure he was okay. I stood in the middle of the finishers' area, staring into the crowd, in awe. I was more proud of Jed in that moment than I had ever been before. His body was beaten so badly in the bike and the first half of the marathon that, had the roles been reversed (and they easily could have been), I'm almost certain that I wouldn't have made it. He drew some awful luck with a bad day and still finished the most brutal of races imaginable.

To do something like this on my own would be an emotional roller coaster. Each finish line brings with it some magic that you previously didn't know existed, and that in and of itself makes me all misty-eyed every time, but being lucky enough to be doing it with my family? That's special.

Unforgettable moments like these are what you gain by

pushing yourself to the limit—whatever your own personal limit may be. If you live your whole life in a comfortable place, you'll never experience those moments that inspire you, that make you tear up with happiness, or that make you overcome with emotion. If you push yourself and you fail, you won't regret trying. But if you push yourself and succeed, you'll experience a feeling of accomplishment and pride that you'll never forget.

▶ READER QUESTION

"Ben, how do you deal with injuries?"

In the second half of 2010, I trained hard for the Las Vegas Marathon. We were just coming off our first Ironman, I was in the best shape of my life, and I wanted to push as hard as I could for my fourth full marathon. I wanted to see just how fast I could run 26.2 miles. It paid off to the tune of a 4:05 marathon, but a day or so after the race, my right knee started to hurt. It was stiff, sore, and I couldn't run on it.

I took marathon recovery to the max and didn't do anything for the first month. I was happy enough—I had PR'ed, it was the holidays, it was cold outside, and relaxing after a solid year of training sounded like a nice Christmas gift to myself. But a short training run a few days after Christmas let me know I was dealing with something a little more serious. The pain hadn't gone away.

I didn't have health insurance at the time, so I prescribed some more rest and icing of the knee. I tested it out gently every couple of weeks and it slowly got better. I was restless and moody and ready to get back on the road, but injuries sometimes take time, and these are the times when you have to be careful.

When the body is hurt, the mind hurts right along with it. You go to a bad place, not knowing how long you're going to be out for. It's obvious that you're going to lose some fitness when you take time off, but I've found that it's also extremely difficult to keep your diet on track, as well. Once you lose the time that you would have spent running, you turn to the habits of old to occupy your time. Focus the energy you usually spend running on maintaining a healthy diet.

Make it a game; make it fun somehow. And find ways to keep up with some physical activity. It's crucial that you put effort on finding active things you can do to pacify yourself as you recuperate. Hurt knee? Work your upper body. Plantar fasciitis? Train in a pool. Find alternative low-impact exercises that you can do for thirty to forty-five minutes a day. Hit the weights. Talk to a trainer. Maintain an active lifestyle that fits with your injury and, if you have health insurance, talk to a doctor.

The biggest thing, though, is to actively work to avoid injury by taking a couple of days off when you first feel the tweak. Make sure to warm up with some jogging before you take off on your sprint workouts. Do some light stretching before and after your workouts and ice when you're recovering. Don't try to do races that you're not ready for like I did. I've been fairly lucky with just the one knee injury in my budding running career. Working to prevent an injury is the best way to deal with injury.

Reader Testimonial

One day, I just decided to do it. Since October of 2010, I've lost nearly ninety pounds and run over twenty different

PUSHING YOURSELF TO THE LIMIT

races, including three half marathons in three weeks this past month. I'm in the middle of my weight-loss journey with about sixty more pounds to lose, but I've definitely been transformed! It's unbelievable that as you realize how physically strong you are, everything else gets stronger, too. I've never felt better, physically, mentally, or emotionally.

The biggest lesson I've learned from running is that losing weight doesn't fix everything, but when you feel strong it's so much easier to deal with the junk that life throws at you. Now I know that I can handle anything. I Do Life. —Stacey S

IRONMAN TRAINING GUIDE

Completing an Ironman may seem impossible, but it's important to understand that any big thing (anything worth doing, that is) is going to seem out of reach at first. If you're looking into competing in an Ironman, you've already come a long way and most likely understand that with the proper training and plan of attack, you will get there and finish the race.

I believe that an Ironman is doable for most people who are in decent shape. It's the idea of an Ironman that scares people off. Let's look at some math, though, and I'll show you how it's possible:

The Ironman cutoff time is a very strict seventeen hours. Let's give you one hour and fifty minutes to complete the swim portion of the race. If you aren't familiar with swim pacing, this is a pretty achievable two minutes and thirty seconds per hundred yards. (Most gym pools are twenty-five yards.) I encourage you to go to a local pool and swim the hundred yards to see just how doable this pace is.

Next we have a 112-mile bike ride, which is a very long ride. Let's give you eight hours to do it. You're looking at fourteen miles per hour, which, granted, is a decent clip, but it's totally doable. By this point in your running/triathlon career, you should be able to maintain this pace pretty easily for at least short distances, and your next five or six months of training will improve your speed even more.

Now let's give you ten minutes during each transition, and you're left with six hours and fifty minutes to run/walk a marathon. That's totally doable. You'll only need to average a 15:39/mile (3.8 miles per hour) pace, which is really only a fast walk/very slow jog, and you'll have completed the Ironman in the allotted time.

When you break it down mathwise, it seems deceptively easy. Don't take it lightly. You're going to have to bust your ass training, and that's how you're going to be prepared.

Training Guide

The following training guide is put together under the assumption that you feel confident running a marathon. It's also wise to get a few shorter-distance triathlons under your belt before you take it on. It is a twenty-five-week guide, giving you a solid six months of training. Your peak training weeks will take you up to fifteen to twenty hours of training (with your longest days on the weekends), so you're going to need to commit to the lifestyle and have systems in place to help lessen the burden on you and those who will be picking up some of your responsibilities while you train.

If you have a family, this will need to be a total team effort and the decisions will need to be talked through in advance to help make the dream a reality without causing a divorce. When you're done, though, the whole family will bask in your achievement. It is an incredible moment for everyone when that finish line is crossed.

WEEK ONE

DAY ONE: run 30 minutes

DAY TWO: swim 1,200 meters

DAY THREE: ride 50 minutes

DAY FOUR: run 20 minutes, swim 20 minutes

DAY FIVE: rest

DAY SIX: run 80 minutes

DAY SEVEN: swim 1,200 meters, bike 60 minutes

WEEK TWO

DAY ONE: run 45 minutes

DAY TWO: ride 60 minutes

DAY THREE: swim 1,400 meters

DAY FOUR: bike 45 minutes, run 20 minutes

DAY FIVE: rest

DAY SIX: ride 120 minutes

DAY SEVEN: swim 1,600 meters

WEEK THREE

DAY ONE: swim 1,500 meters, run 20 minutes

DAY TWO: bike 80 minutes

DAY THREE: run 60 minutes

DAY FOUR: run 30 minutes, bike 45 minutes

ironman training guide

PUSHING YOURSELF TO THE LIMIT

DAY FIVE: rest

DAY SIX: bike 120 minutes, run 20 minutes

DAY SEVEN: swim 1,600 meters open water

WEEK FOUR

DAY ONE: stretch and rest

DAY TWO: run 80 minutes

DAY THREE: swim 2,000 meters

DAY FOUR: bike 60 minutes, run 30 minutes

DAY FIVE: rest

DAY SIX: bike 150 minutes

DAY SEVEN: swim 2,000 meters, run 20 minutes

WEEK FIVE

DAY ONE: run 90 minutes

DAY TWO: swim 1,200 meters, run 30 minutes

DAY THREE: ride 60 minutes

DAY FOUR: run 80 minutes

DAY FIVE: rest

DAY SIX: ride 200 minutes

DAY SEVEN: swim 1,600 meters, run 20 minutes

WEEK SIX

DAY ONE: run 90 minutes

DAY TWO: swim 1,600 meters

DAY THREE: ride 60 minutes, run 30 minutes

DAY FOUR: run 50 minutes

DAY FIVE: rest

DAY SIX: ride 200 minutes, swim 800 meters

DAY SEVEN: run 120 minutes

WEEK SEVEN

DAY ONE: ride 75 minutes

DAY TWO: rest

DAY THREE: ride 75 minutes, run 25 minutes

DAY FOUR: ride 75 minutes

DAY FIVE: rest

DAY SIX: swim 2,500 meters, run 30 minutes

DAY SEVEN: run 120 minutes

WEEK EIGHT

DAY ONE: swim 2,000 meters

DAY TWO: ride 90 minutes

DAY THREE: run 80 minutes

DAY FOUR: ride 90 minutes

ironman training guide

DAY FIVE: rest

DAY SIX: ride 200 minutes, run 30 minutes

DAY SEVEN: swim 2,000 meters

WEEK NINE

DAY ONE: run 100 minutes

DAY TWO: ride 100 minutes

DAY THREE: swim 1,600 meters, run 20 minutes

DAY FOUR: ride 120 minutes

DAY FIVE: rest

DAY SIX: swim 3,200 meters

DAY SEVEN: run 120 minutes, swim 1,000 meters

WEEK TEN

DAY ONE: run 100 minutes

DAY TWO: ride 120 minutes

DAY THREE: swim 2,000 meters

DAY FOUR: ride 150 minutes

DAY FIVE: rest

DAY SIX: ride 240 minutes

DAY SEVEN: swim 2,400 meters open water

WEEK ELEVEN

DAY ONE: run 50 minutes

DAY TWO: ride 120 minutes

DAY THREE: ride 120 minutes

DAY FOUR: swim 2,500 meters

DAY FIVE: rest

DAY SIX: run 130 minutes

DAY SEVEN: ride 150 minutes

WEEK TWELVE

DAY ONE: run 75 minutes

DAY TWO: ride 120 minutes

DAY THREE: ride 100 minutes, swim 1,600 meters

DAY FOUR: swim 2,000 meters

DAY FIVE: rest

DAY SIX: run 140 minutes

DAY SEVEN: ride 180 minutes

WEEK THIRTEEN

DAY ONE: run 80 minutes

DAY TWO: swim 2,500 meters

DAY THREE: ride 120 minutes, run 30 minutes

DAY FOUR: run 50 minutes

ironman training guide

PUSHING YOURSELF TO THE LIMIT

DAY FIVE: rest

DAY SIX: ride 260 minutes

DAY SEVEN: run 80 minutes, swim 2,000 meters

WEEK FOURTEEN

DAY ONE: ride 100 minutes

DAY TWO: swim 3,600 meters

DAY THREE: run 50 minutes, swim 1,200 meters

DAY FOUR: ride 120 minutes

DAY FIVE: rest

DAY SIX: run 140 minutes

DAY SEVEN: ride 200 minutes

WEEK FIFTEEN

DAY ONE: run 90 minutes

DAY TWO: ride 150 minutes

DAY THREE: swim 3,600 meters

DAY FOUR: ride 120 minutes, run 30 minutes

DAY FIVE: rest

DAY SIX: ride 260 minutes

DAY SEVEN: run 90 minutes

WEEK SIXTEEN

DAY ONE: rest

DAY TWO: swim 3,000 meters

DAY THREE: run 100 minutes

DAY FOUR: ride 150 minutes

DAY FIVE: rest

DAY SIX: ride 200 minutes, run 40 minutes

DAY SEVEN: swim 2,000 meters

WEEK SEVENTEEN

DAY ONE: ride 140 minutes

DAY TWO: run 40 minutes, swim 1,600 meters

DAY THREE: ride 100 minutes, swim 1,600 meters

DAY FOUR: run 60 minutes

DAY FIVE: rest

DAY SIX: ride 300 minutes

DAY SEVEN: swim 4,000 meters

WEEK EIGHTEEN

DAY ONE: run 100 minutes

DAY TWO: ride 100 minutes

DAY THREE: swim 3,000 meters

DAY FOUR: ride 60 minutes, run 60 minutes

ironman training guide

DAY FIVE: rest

DAY SIX: run 150 minutes

DAY SEVEN: ride 180 minutes

WEEK NINETEEN

DAY ONE: ride 75 minutes, run 60 minutes

DAY TWO: ride 100 minutes

DAY THREE: run 110 minutes

DAY FOUR: swim 2,500 meters

DAY FIVE: rest

DAY SIX: ride 180 minutes, run 40 minutes

DAY SEVEN: swim 2,000 meters, run 50 minutes

WEEK TWENTY

DAY ONE: ride 150 minutes

DAY TWO: run 70 minutes, swim 2,000 meters

DAY THREE: ride 100 minutes

DAY FOUR: run 85 minutes

DAY FIVE: rest

DAY SIX: ride 360 minutes

DAY SEVEN: swim 4,000 meters

WEEK TWENTY-ONE

DAY ONE: run 50 minutes

DAY TWO: ride 150 minutes

DAY THREE: swim 3,200 meters, run 40 minutes

DAY FOUR: ride 120 minutes

DAY FIVE: rest

DAY SIX: run 170 minutes

DAY SEVEN: ride 200 minutes

WEEK TWENTY-TWO

DAY ONE: run 80 minutes

DAY TWO: ride 180 minutes

DAY THREE: ride 100 minutes, run 40 minutes

DAY FOUR: swim 4,000 meters

DAY FIVE: rest

DAY SIX: ride 360 minutes, run 50 minutes

DAY SEVEN: swim 2,000 meters

WEEK TWENTY-THREE

DAY ONE: run 75 minutes

DAY TWO: ride 100 minutes, swim 3,600 meters

DAY THREE: run 75 minutes

DAY FOUR: ride 120 minutes

ironman training guide

DAY FIVE: rest

DAY SIX: run 100 minutes

DAY SEVEN: rest

WEEK TWENTY-FOUR

DAY ONE: ride 70 minutes

DAY TWO: ride 50 minutes

DAY THREE: swim 20 minutes

DAY FOUR: rest

DAY FIVE: run 30 minutes

DAY SIX: rest

DAY SEVEN: swim 20 minutes

WEEK TWENTY-FIVE

DAY ONE: run 20 minutes

DAY TWO: ride 20 minutes

DAY THREE: rest

DAY FOUR: rest

DAY FIVE: walk/jog 15 minutes

DAY SIX: rest

DAY SEVEN: RACE!

9

maintaining your lifestyle

aS EXCITED AS I was to be an Ironman, I was even more excited that we weren't going to go to Chili's and immediately talk ourselves into doing something bigger. Life isn't a race, and it certainly isn't a competition. It's a journey, and in order to be successful, you need to live your life to the fullest even when you're not testing or pushing yourself to the limits. As I met goal after goal throughout my journey, my ultimate goal shifted from a lower number on the scale or a higher level of fitness to an entirely new lifestyle that included fitness, healthy eating, adventures, and love.

All goals need to be treated this way in order for you to be truly successful. If you live your life on a constant mission to check the next great thing off your to-do list, you might miss some of the joy in the in-between moments. You know as well as I do that it doesn't matter what car we drive or how many followers we have on Twitter. Life isn't about the size of your boat or the number of zeros on your paycheck. We weren't put on this planet to impress our coworkers with our latest and greatest superphone. And the truth is that we're not even here to count how many miles we've run or collect medals from races. I believe that we're here to find our own happiness and spread it around through the things that we do—whether that's running together, laughing together, or just being together.

I found my spark in running, and maybe you will, too. But running, just like every other hobby, is a means to an end—or, as is often the case, ends. The ends with running are too many to count—a healthier body, sharper mind, an easy way to blow off steam, and a common bond between friends, to start. It shapes my life and helps me live my life as well as I can.

We can't run twenty-four hours a day, and yet we need to live with that spark at every moment, or else it might burn out. Keeping that spark burning when we're at the grocery store, going on a date, or even sitting in a cubicle takes just as much effort as the running itself, and is equally important. It's a way of maintaining all the benefits that running—or whatever it is that gives you your smile—has to offer.

Of course, diet and exercise are integral parts of maintaining a healthy lifestyle when you're not training for a particular race. When I think about maintaining weight, I always think about my college campus. The campus was beautiful and meticulously organized, which was a stark contrast to my life at the time. When I got depressed by the dank clutter of my own room and existence, I would go outside and enjoy the order and beauty of the grounds and buildings that were so fastidiously maintained.

Going back even further in my spotty academic career, I can clearly recall the concept of entropy from a high school science class. The principle of entropy is that any natural system will tend toward disorder if left unchecked. If a veritable army of maintenance workers and gardeners hadn't constantly expended huge amounts of energy, the college campus that I found so beautiful would have quickly fallen into disrepair.

This same principle guides my life today when it comes to my weight and overall health. I worked so hard to get where I am, by eating right and exercising in order to reach my goals. I didn't realize how much energy it would take to maintain this new order of things until I found myself in between races and I quickly started slipping back into the natural disorder of myself—the lazy, overfed, and poorly maintained version of me that I'd worked so hard to change.

A huge part of the problem is that our society has created a difficult environment in which to maintain a healthy lifestyle. We've worked hard as a species to find easier ways of doing things, to the point that it now requires no effort whatsoever to eat whatever we want, whenever we want it. We don't have to chase down our meat, grow our own vegetables, walk around and pick nuts and berries, or even wait for the particular berry that we want to be in season. We can be totally inert and consume all the calories that we want, having instant gratification without any effort at all.

In addition, we have created new types of foods that are instantly gratifying and addictive. Not only can we sit around and eat whatever we want, but the majority of the things that most of us eat build fat, rob us of energy, and leave us wanting more. It's no coincidence that every convenience store in America sells cereals, chips, candy, cookies, and ice cream instead of fresh produce. They sell them because that's what we've decided to eat. It's no accident that there are more types of ice cream and frozen pizzas in the freezers of grocery stores than there are types of vegetables in the produce section. These foods require no preparation,

are easier to eat and digest, and feed our addictions to fats and sugars.

I realize that this all comes as a surprise to precisely no one. We all know what is healthy and what we should be eating to be well nourished, avoid becoming obese, or lose the extra weight that we've already gained. The challenge is to actually do it and then to maintain it, and that requires new ways of doing things.

I spoke earlier about my dad's concept of acting your way into right thinking when it comes to beating addiction and living life to the fullest. Well, the exact same thing applies to food. Once I started preparing and eating the right foods, my thinking came around and I started to enjoy those healthy foods. I acted my way out of the instant gratification mind-set and into the much more enjoyable mode of learning about what to eat and why, how to shop for it, how to cook it, and how to eat it. I replaced the mindless activity of simply feeding my addictions by becoming engaged in the art and science of nourishing myself.

Now I take so much more pleasure in the act of preparing a Moroccan tagine or a fresh soup than I ever did in popping a frozen pizza in the oven or going through the drive-through at a fast food restaurant. But I didn't think my way into this. I had to take the actions first—finding recipes, shopping, slicing, dicing, sautéing, and eating until I found the joy. I had to act my way into healthy thinking and healthy eating.

I GENERALLY START my day with a run, followed by a smoothie and toast with peanut butter. Here are a couple of my favorite smoothie recipes:

MEEMAW'S SUPER BLUEBERRY SMOOTHIE

Combine the following ingredients and blend until smooth:

- 1 tablespoon almond butter
- ¼ cup silken tofu
- ½ cup soy milk
- ½ cup water
- 1 teaspoon flaxseeds
- 1 tablespoon flaxseed oil (optional)
- ½ banana
- ½–¾ cup frozen blueberries

TROPICAL SMOOTHIE

Combine and blend until smooth:

- 1 cup skim, soy, or almond milk
- ¼ cup 2 percent vanilla yogurt
- ½ cup frozen kiwis
- 1 frozen banana
- 1 tablespoon peanut butter
- 1 squirt chocolate syrup (optional)
- ¼ cup frozen mango chunks
- ¼ cup frozen pineapple chunks

For lunch, you can't go wrong with soup. This is one of my favorite soup recipes:

BLACK BEAN SOUP

In a large soup pot or saucepan over medium-high heat, cook 5 slices of bacon, diced, until about halfway done (4 or 5 minutes). Add 2 medium onions, diced, and cook for another 4 minutes or so, stirring often. (Note: You can skip the bacon and just start by cooking the diced onions in 2 or 3 tablespoons of olive oil.)

Add about 6 cloves of garlic, pressed or chopped finely, and cook for another minute or two. Add 2 cups of chicken or vegetable stock, 2 cups of canned chopped tomatoes with their juice, 2 cans of drained but not rinsed black beans, and 2 teaspoons cumin. Bring to a boil over medium-high heat, stirring often.

Turn down to a simmer, and cook about 10 minutes, stirring occasionally. Top with roughly chopped cilantro, fat-free sour cream, shredded cheddar, and a few chopped scallions.

ROASTED VEGETABLES

For dinner, I often chop up whatever vegetables I have in the fridge (my favorite combination is broccoli, carrots, potatoes, sweet potatoes, and cauliflower) into approximately ¾-inch pieces, and add them to a cookie sheet with sides (a.k.a. a jelly roll pan) along with a chopped onion and several whole peeled garlic cloves. I then drizzle olive oil over the vegetables, season them generously with salt and pepper, and mix it all together with my hands. This goes in a 450-degree oven, on an upper rack, for 20 minutes. I give them a good stir and then roast for another 20 minutes or so. You can eat this on its own or along with any healthy fish or chicken entrée for a perfectly balanced meal.

You don't have to go on a crash diet or become a professional chef in order to achieve this radical change in thinking. I don't want you to use a busy schedule or ineptitude in the kitchen as an excuse not to eat well. All you have to do is change your actions, whether that means becoming knowledgeable about calories and ordering the right things at restaurants or snacking on fresh fruits and vegetables from the grocery store rather than something from the convenience store. Don't use the excuse that you don't like those foods. You will undoubtedly grow to like those things as you grow to like the results and the person you become. We act our way into right thinking.

Moderation is really hard, especially when it comes to food, because even though eating poorly is often an addiction, it's not like other addictions where the only real solution is to stop the behavior entirely. While you can completely quit gambling or smoking or drinking, you can't simply quit eating. You do have to moderate it if you want to lose weight and be healthy. (The same thing goes for people on the other end of the spectrum, which is why eating disorders such as anorexia are so difficult to successfully treat.) Food is the one thing we can get addicted to that we literally need to survive. It's incredibly difficult to eat just enough to fuel our bodies, because we're conditioned to feed ourselves not just when we're hungry, but when we're bored, depressed, lonely, angry, happy, or tired, as well.

Very few drug addicts or alcoholics are able to achieve a balance when it comes to using their addictive substance. It's all or nothing. The saying "Once you've become a pickle, you can't ever be a cucumber again" sums it up pretty well. With food, though, you have to learn to moderate. You must somehow find a way to unpickle yourself.

The trick with food, I've found, is not subscribing to a so-called diet, but just being a smarter eater. We all know that grilled chicken should take the place of a McWhatever and that an English muffin with a little peanut butter on it is a better breakfast than half a box of Fruity Pebbles. This is, of course, easier said than done, so we have to figure out a way to put a healthy plan into action. When you do, please let me know. I'll readily admit that there are still days (okay, weeks) when I grab that blueberry scone or sneak into the kitchen for some late night popcorn. Diet is my Achilles' heel. My battle against my food addiction will be a lifelong struggle, and I've accepted that.

People often ask me whether dieting or exercise is more important to maintaining my weight. Although so much of my journey has focused on running, the maintenance part is all about the food. Of course, they go hand in hand, but eating right "outweighs" exercise when it comes to maintaining a healthy weight. The reason for this is that I would have to exercise excessively all the time in order to make up for the extended, uncontrolled bouts of attack eating that I am prone to. It's simply easier to eat fewer calories than to try burning so many calories after the fact.

Luckily, when you become a runner, eating more than a regular person is not only necessary, but it's encouraged. As you work yourself through the distances, you'll be training more and more and you'll need more and more calories to supplement your workload. A two-hundred-pound male running for an hour at a ten-minute-per-mile average pace will burn roughly a thousand calories. And somehow, the fact that you now need to eat extra food makes it less tempting. It's no longer illicit and tempting. By running, I've therefore found a way to use food the way humans are meant to—as fuel.

For a runner, your goal should be to fuel your body with enough of the right foods to optimize your performance. To that end, you'll need to eliminate the things that will slow you down and inhibit your recovery. In doing this, you'll become a healthier eater and in turn a healthier person. You'll act your way into a healthier relationship with food.

runner's guide to nutrition

MY PERSONAL TRAINER, Suzanne, helped me come up with this list of the top ten components of a runner's diet:

1. Water

You have to be well hydrated to run and to lose weight. Ideally, water should be the only thing you drink. I understand how difficult this can be for some people (like me), but you really must try to get a large percentage of your liquids from water.

2. Omega-3s

Go for fatty fish such as tuna or salmon, or take a fish oil supplement, instead. Omega-3s will keep your joints lubricated, which is very important as you pound the pavement on said joints. Omega-3s also lower your risk of heart disease and arthritis and have been shown to prevent Alzheimer's disease.

3. Calcium

Strong bones equal strong runners. Go-to calcium sources for runners include Greek yogurt, tofu, chickpeas, and milk. Calcium also helps your nerves and muscles function well.

4. Protein

Protein helps your muscles recover, and you're going to need plenty of it as you train for that next big race. Lean meats (turkey, chicken, and fish), eggs, peanut butter, and tofu are good protein sources. They'll help you increase your muscle mass, ensure that your immune system functions well, and maintain healthy hair, skin, and nails.

5. Potassium

Potassium helps your muscles and nerves function properly and restores the level of electrolytes in your body, which is important after strenuous exercise to prevent headaches or fainting. Go for some bananas to get your potassium going. During and after a run is my banana time.

6. Vitamin C

Beef up your immune system to prevent illnesses and help your body absorb the iron that you have ingested. Oranges!

7. Spirulina

This vegetarian product comes in a powder and contains all essential amino acids, is rich in GLA (which is good for healthy skin and allegedly prevents wrinkles!), and acts as a bit of a detox product for your blood if you have been ingesting sugary or salty foods.

8. Fiber

Fruits, vegetables, and oatmeal are awesome for losing weight, as you feel fuller faster and longer. That means no more reaching for unnecessary snacks! Fiber ensures that your digestive system is working in tip-top shape so that your intestines absorb all the nutrients from your foods and your body can actually utilize everything that you're eating.

9. Multivitamins

These are important to fill in any potential gaps in your diet.

10. Carbohydrates and Fats!

I saved the best for last, but (sorry), I don't mean the

"fun" kind of carbs and fats in Pringles and Pop-Tarts. Runners need fuel from the "good" fats and complex carbs in the form of whole grains, fruits, veggies, and the occasional pasta dish. As far as fats go, stick with the unsaturated fats in nuts and avocados.

General helpful hint—When in doubt, eat more fish.

Although I do consider diet to be the most important element in maintaining a healthy lifestyle, exercise now remains a huge part of my life even when I'm not in training. It's astonishing how once exercising is a part of your life and you have a good routine, you begin to crave it. Of course, this doesn't happen at first, but it generally only takes a few weeks to activate that desire to stick with the plan of attack. . Maybe it's the endorphin addiction kicking in and replacing your old, destructive addictions, but before long you start to look forward to that daily run or boot camp session just like you used to look forward to your after-work drink or late-night cereal binge.

This is why it's so important to replace your unhealthy addictions with healthy ones. If you have a solid workout regimen in place, you'll have something to turn to when you're feeling antsy or bored. Not only that, but you'll have something that you'll look forward to doing, and you'll start to look forward to the feeling of satisfaction that comes after a good workout. Without a healthy plan to take the place of your vices, you'll end up feeling empty and useless (at best) or be tempted to go back to your old ways (at worst).

YOU NEED A strong core to be a strong runner, so get familiar with these workout terms:

Planking: Get into a sort of push-up position but rather than your hands, use your elbows, forearms, and wrists to support your upper body and toes on the lower body. Just hold yourself there. Push your butt into the air a little bit. (Your body shouldn't be exactly straight from toe to head; you want a very slight tent situation going.)

Side planks: Put your elbow down with your lower body resting on alternating side-of-foot, with your body facing out and your other hand sticking into the air.

Butt-balance torso turners: (I'm sure there's an actual term for this.) Balance on your butt with your knees bent and your feet in the air. Keep your back and shoulders at a forty-five-degree angle. Clasp your hands together and move them from hip to hip while maintaining your balance and not letting your feet touch the ground.

Leg scissors: Lie flat on your back. Keeping your legs straight, lift them twelve or so inches into the air, and scissor them, alternating up and down.

(Also, YouTube is your friend when looking for the exact forms and processes with these exercises.)

In addition to abdominal exercises, here are some of my favorite workouts that I use to accompany my running:

Lunges: With your hands on your hips, step out with alternating legs. Bend your back knee to nearly-touching-the floor, bend your front knee, and back up.

Suicide sprints: Place a mark at ten yards, twenty yards, and thirty yards. Sprint to the ten and back, then the twenty and back, then the thirty and back.

Burpees: Hit the deck onto your hands and toes, do a push-up, push yourself back up and jump, hands up, into the air. Repeat.

Body squats: Stand with your feet a shoulder width apart and squat down, push your butt out behind you, and rise back up.

Wall sits: Do a sort of squat but keep your back up against the wall and hold it. Your legs should be bent at a ninety-degree angle or somewhere close to that.

Push-ups: You should know what push-ups are.

Jumping jacks: And these, too.

The trick is to combine all sorts of these exercises into one big fifteen-to-twenty-minute boot camp workout. For best results, go outside or to your local track to do these. You'll feel like a badass out there tearing it up. Take a lot of water.

For example, here is one of my "favorite" circuits:

50 jumping jacks
45-second plank
8 burpees
30 seconds of leg scissors
4 suicide sprints
10 push-ups
Repeat 4x for a total of 5 rounds.

Mix and match or add your own tried-and-true exercise. Just make sure to push hard. The idea is that these are short-ish timewise, but challenging intensity-wise.

MAINTAINING YOUR LIFESTYLE

For maintenance workouts, I stick mostly to running, but I throw in regular swimming sessions roughly twice a week to spice up the routine. Swimming eight hundred to a thousand yards twice a week really refreshes me. When you're not upping the ante by training for a race, you need to find ways to keep exercising fun so that you aren't tempted to slack off. You can easily do this by mixing things up and trying new exercises, classes, and workouts, even in very small increments.

My fiancée and I have regular push-up and planking competitions for fifteen to twenty minutes once every few days to make sure that our muscles stay toned. She's also really into ab workouts, so I join her in those once a week or so. Each of these little sessions adds up throughout the weeks, and when I started to tally it all together, I realized that I'm doing a couple of hours of bonus workouts in addition to my regular regimen, which is very motivating and satisfying.

▶ READER QUESTION

"What do you suggest for people that don't have time to work out?"

Here's the thing: I, Ben Davis, am the king of excuses. I've skipped working out claiming a proper observance of daylight saving. I've prayed and prayed for a flat tire to get out of a particularly excruciating bike ride. I've skipped runs because the terrorist threat level reached orange. If there is a reason to avoid exertion, I can find it. At the end of the day, though, I'll readily admit I just didn't feel like exercising.

It's simple math. Let's work out some numbers. Let's say you sleep seven hours and work nine. Throw in an hour of travel and you've used seventeen hours so far. Add another three hours for showering, dressing, and taking care of your kids, and two more for meals. That's twenty-two hours. Give yourself an hour of mindless TV and/or catching up with Facebook and Twitter, and, voilà, you still have an hour to sweat it out.

If, however, you inventory every single hour and still can't find thirty or forty-five minutes to go for a jog, working out isn't your biggest problem—either time management or support from your family is. Every single time my brother crosses a finish line, it's the culmination of three or four months of strict training. He puts in the miles just like every other finisher, and he does so as the head high school football coach in SEC. In the South. Oh, and he has two children younger than four and a wife. He spends hours and hours every day breaking down film, game planning, teaching math, and coaching, but he still finds time to squeeze in the workouts. If he can do it, anyone can.

When all is said and done, it comes down to prioritizing and whether or not you actually want it. We make time for the things that are important to us, and perhaps running isn't what you really want. That's totally fine. It's your business. But don't hide behind the "don't have time" excuse. The biggest part about breaking through excuses is identifying the ones that plague you, the ones you involuntarily reach for when deciding whether or not to go out for a run. These are all too similar to the lies you tell yourself and others about how you're really doing, what you ate last night, and what you really want out of life. Once you refuse to give yourself an excuse for not working out, you'll suddenly find the time to do it. It will become a part of your daily life that you would never dream of skipping, a way of maintaining your health and your sanity, and you'll naturally fit it into your routine without giving it a second thought.

do life

On November 6, 2011, I had surgery to remove my thyroid because of a nodule growing on the right side of the thyroid. On November 8, 2011, my world changed forever. I went to the surgeon for the routine post-op visit. He told me the pathology report came back and the nodule was cancer. It really didn't hit me until I got in the car and my husband of less than six months was driving me home. I had cancer!

I knew immediately that I had to do something to make a change for my life and also for others. As I was resting in bed for the next few days, I began to ponder what I could do that would benefit me and others. I decided to start running and raise money for the American Cancer Society. My grandfather, who was one of the most important men in my life, was diagnosed with brain cancer in the late 1980s and died from it in 1992. I wanted to run for his memory and for my survival.

Once my body felt up to moving again, I started back slowly in the gym. In January, I started a running plan through an online group and also joined the Tumblr community. Both groups were quintessential to my daily motivation. As I read everyone's successes and sympathized with their struggles, I gained strength and confidence that I could be successful with running. I signed up for the DetermiNation fund-raising group with the American Cancer Society and committed myself to running the half marathon in Nashville, Tennessee.

After more than three and a half months of waking up early, getting home late, and running in strange places, I completed my first half marathon on April 28, 2012, in two hours and fifty-seven minutes. In the process, I made a lot of lifelong friends, raised more than thirteen hundred dollars for the American Cancer Society, and lost fifteen pounds. I am already thinking about what race I can enter next and how I can get my husband motivated to change his lifestyle and start running alongside me. —Kelly R

spreading the smile

WHEN YOU START living your life to the fullest, a funny thing happens. Instead of considering yourself more important than ever with your fancy new physique and positive outlook on life, you come to realize that you are actually just one small (or at least smaller) person and there is a big, beautiful world out there that is filled with people who are just as important as you. Your life, in fact, isn't that big a deal. That thing that your boss said to you the other day that pissed you off is relatively insignificant in the grand scheme of things, and having to wait a few extra minutes in line to buy a coffee really isn't the end of the world.

I'm so much stronger having dealt with my obesity and the mind-set that came from it. My depression and my weight once permeated every single part of my life. I blamed my weight on one hundred percent of my shortcomings. If a girl broke up with me or rejected me, I assumed that it was because I was fat. If my professor didn't like my essay, I assumed he simply didn't like me because I was fat. It's a ridiculous game that we addicts play with ourselves, another way that we allow our addictions to rule our lives.

Once you banish that attitude and become more confident, not only do you do better work and become a better person, but you start dealing with problems in a healthier way. Instead of throwing pity parties every time something goes wrong, you work at your shortcomings and find a way to make them better. You stop cutting corners because you actually care about what you're doing and you can't use obesity as an excuse any longer.

The moment I started running, every part of my life got better. It was like a light switch flipping on. My GPA in college rose a full point before I graduated, which never would have been possible had I not gotten my life under control. I had been on track to flunk out or else quit school altogether. I was majoring in journalism, and when I was obese and depressed, I was content to satisfy my on-air credits by doing audio or something equally reclusive, but just three months into my turnaround I went out and did something scary. I auditioned to be an anchor for the college news telecast. It was exciting and risky to put actual effort into my work instead of just doing the bare minimum that was needed to get by. I got the part, spent two days a week on television, and, of course, that motivated me to keep going.

This, of course, is called perspective. I've found that the more full of self-hatred you are, the more overblown your ego becomes. Your insecurities and addictions fuel this belief that everything wrong in the world or in your life is all about you and your problems. You may think that once your life turns around, your attitude will do a perfect 180 and you'll start to believe that everything right in the world is about you, too, but in fact an even more dramatic change is more likely to occur. With the perspective that comes with

a healthy mind and body, you realize that even the best parts of your life are insignificant unless you can find a way to share your newfound spark with the rest of the world.

Once you get further along in your journey and reach many of your own personal goals, the best way to stay motivated is to find something new and work as hard as possible to get it. This can be a huge triathlon, a destination race, or something apart from racing entirely—a new relationship, say, a new volunteer effort, or your own new way of sharing your smile. In this way, the effort that you put in will become just as enjoyable as the outcome, and you'll begin to find pleasure in the journey.

This enjoyment that you'll start to feel from running itself can be described as runner's high or a certain euphoria that will start to come from running. Runner's high for me is when, after a couple of miles, everything in the world just seems . . . better. All of a sudden, the pounding on the pavement throughout my body doesn't feel like pounding anymore. It becomes a rhythmic dance. My breathing relaxes and I'm just gliding. But that's just the beginning. After the physical runner's high, I find myself thinking about writing, or a cool idea for a video, or a good idea for the Do Life movement. I begin to get creative and find myself wishing I had a pen and paper to write down my ideas. It's completely different from the adrenaline rush of gambling or the fleeting comfort that comes from eating lots of food. It's an exhilarating, creative, more positive high, and it usually lasts all day.

Since turning my life around, I've done some pretty cool things. I've run marathons in six different states and three different countries. I've climbed mountains, swum in oceans, and done a twelve-hour adventure race in the wilderness of central Tennessee. I've been on the cover of

Runner's World and exchanged e-mails with John Mayer. The harder I've worked, the more I've gotten out of life, and the further I've spread my smile, the more it's come back to me.

In late 2010, a fitness center about twenty miles north of Chicago invited me to come speak at the kickoff event for their new weight-loss program. It occurred to me that while I was near the big city, I should invite people to meet up at Millennium Park and run a few miles together. In response, I received an e-mail from a girl named Brooke. She mentioned that she'd like to do the run but she would be busy that day. She wanted to know if we were going to meet up again while I was in town for another run. But as I had a flight back home to catch after the run, that would be my only chance. She wrote back, "It was worth a shot. Have fun! Peace and happy running." I promptly forgot that the exchange ever happened.

The weekend I was in the Windy City, there was a blizzard. My flight was pushed back, and we were forced to push back the run, too. Brooke was in town for two weeks from Vancouver, and ended up making it to the rescheduled run. It was still dumping snow, so only four of us met up that day. What was supposed to be a 5K turned into an incredibly beautiful (and cold) five-mile run through Chicago. Afterward, we warmed up at a nearby Caribou Coffee. Brooke and I kept talking. It's truly amazing how life rewards you when you start to make the effort. If you put yourself out there and put good things into the world, they come back to you tenfold. To this day, Brooke puts up with me with the occasional roll of the eyes and sarcastic grin. When I'm lying in bed not feeling up to a particular run, she pushes me out the door. When I hit an eating rut, we make some roasted vegetables together. And we run.

ONE GREAT WAY to spread the smile that comes with running is to sign up for a race that benefits a charity. It's hard not to get inspired when you run one of these races. The people you'll meet are amazing. Some of them have survived horrible diseases and have gone on to run marathons or complete Ironmans. Other people who run these races do so in honor of a loved one who has passed away from the disease they are running for. These races spread awareness and raise money for important causes. It doesn't get much better than that.

Don't be afraid to ask your friends and coworkers to support you in the race. This is part of going public with your new lifestyle and all your struggles. You'll be surprised how many people will show up and sponsor you when they hear about the good things you are doing.

The other benefit of running for a cause is that you'll meet running buddies who are passionate about the same things as you. If you're not into joining one of these races, you can also find your own way to benefit others through running. I haven't done much in the way of charity running, but we've done some cool things with our organization, such as natural disaster relief efforts, teen depression/suicide awareness, and cancer fund-raising.

Here is a list of some of the biggest charity races around the country:

AIDS Walk—a 10K to benefit AIDS research around the
   world
www.aidswalk.net
Walk Like MADD—a 5K to raise funds for Mothers
   Against Drunk Driving
www.support.madd.org

Walk to Defeat ALS—150 walks around the country to
support ALS research and patient service programs
www.alsa.org/walk

Alzheimer's Association Memory Walk—six hundred
walks each year to raise money to end Alzheimer's
www.alz.org/memorywalk

Walk for a Cure: Arthritis Foundation—choose either a
one- or three-mile course to benefit arthritis research
www.arthritis.org

Cupid's Chase—a 5K to raise funds for people with
disabilities
www.comop.org/cupidschase

Walk Now for Autism Speaks—an international event to
generate funds for autism research and awareness
www.autismspeaks.org

Komen Race for the Cure Series—the largest series of
5Ks in the world to raise funds and awareness for
the fight against breast cancer
www.komen.org

Relay for Life—an overnight event to raise money for
the American Cancer Society
www.relayforlife.org/relay

American Heart Association's Heart Walk—ranges from
1.6 to six miles to fight heart disease and strokes
www.americanheart.org

The Walk from Obesity—a national walk to raise money
for research, education, prevention, and treatment
of obesity
www.walkfromobesity.com

A few weeks later, my dad and I went to New York to try
the same thing on a slightly larger scale, and fifty people

showed up the night after a blizzard to run in the snow and freezing temperatures with us in Central Park. Afterward, we went across Columbus Circle and ate at a cafeteria. We ate and talked and laughed and shared stories of our successes and our failures in running, weight loss, and life. We had helped a few dozen New Yorkers from all walks of life bond over running, just like we had done. It was an incredible sight to behold. When we finally left a few hours later, we looked at each other and could tell we were all thinking the same thing: we had to spread this smile further.

In early 2011, Jed, Pa, and I came up with the idea for a cross-country tour for our fledgling Do Life enterprise. We would spend the summer traveling from city to city, staging informal 5K runs for anyone who wanted to join us. There would be no pressure to compete, just an atmosphere of fun and camaraderie, the message being that anybody can do this—we can all strive toward a healthier lifestyle, and it can be laid-back and enjoyable. We wanted to take our message to the streets—literally—grassroots-style.

That spring, we traveled to several cities around the country. We visited Seattle in March and got another chance to see how one of our informal 5Ks might work. About thirty-five of us gathered in a light rain and ran along the water, each of us feeling the energy of being involved in something greater than ourselves. It was a perfect example of how we can connect as a group while we're each on a personal journey, and how we can enjoy the many moments along the way, even if we're a long way from achieving our individual goals. That group was a composite of what we would find so many times during our tour that summer. We were a diverse group with a common bond—the desire to lead a healthier life through running and sharing it with others.

When we finally launched a full-fledged Do Life tour,

we had no idea where we would stay on our route, but I figured that some kind soul would offer us a place to stay with the attitude that we're all in this together. But when we announced the tour and the fact that we could use some help in each city with lodging and logistics, we were completely overwhelmed by the number of people who reached out with offers to help. It was amazing.

Just eighteen months earlier, I had been locked in a shell of hopeless desperation, lying to those closest to me and keeping them at arm's length. Now I was living a life that was truly beyond my wildest dreams. By being honest with myself and the people I loved, I was able to create a health and running community that focused on spreading happiness and accountability, and people were going out of their way to help me. And that only served to spread my smile even wider.

It wasn't just me. Running had changed the people around me for the better, and it was an amazing thing to witness. One of the first stops on our tour was in Hattiesburg, Mississippi, and my dad told me about the last time he was in that particular town. It was during the summer of 1980 when he was twenty-three years old and in the depths of his drug addiction, wasting his life away. Since then, he'd turned his life around, and thirty years later, he was back in Hattiesburg with a plan to try and change people's lives for the better. It was pretty inspiring.

I got lucky when Meemaw reached out to me, and again when Jed and Pa joined me on this journey, encouraging me every step of the way. All of us who make it through our addictions are lucky. Someone along the way offers us a way out—but it's up to us to take it. Pa could easily have continued smuggling and doing drugs, but he took action, fought his addictions, and got out. I could have continued my old lifestyle after Meemaw tried to push me in the right direction, but I took action, changed my life, and got out. When your moment arrives and someone tries to help you, accept their offer. You may not get another chance.

Over the course of the next forty days, we met and ran with more than sixteen hundred folks across the country. We met people like Nancy in Buffalo who trained for the 5K by literally running through her house. We met Dawn and Shelly, sisters from New Orleans who have together lost more than 350 pounds and found joy in life. We set our feet in both oceans, dealt with 120-degree heat in Phoenix, and braved a torrential downpour in Minneapolis. We ran with folks in Cleveland and Portland and Orlando, too. We did life in Canada, St. Louis, and San Francisco. We met Katey from Detroit, who not only gave us a couch to crash on and veggie burgers to eat, but gave my dad a first-rate haircut. We drove an SUV from sea to shining sea and forged hundreds of bonds that we won't soon forget.

Three days after the tour, we completed our second Ironman, but that forty-day tour remains the highlight of my life. The joy is indeed in the journey. We may have specific goals in mind—a certain target weight or a distance or race to run—but those goals can't be our sole focal point. There are simply too many other things to be enjoyed along the way. We must open our minds and our senses to all of them, lest we get to the end of our journeys and wonder, *Is this all there is?*

When we set our goals, we should do so under the assumption that happiness will not magically flip on once we hit the goal. We have to strive for something deeper than weight loss, deeper than running a certain race, deeper than giving up the smokes or alcohol or gambling or drugs or whatever it might be that we have to stop. Once we go a little deeper,

that's where we'll find the smile. That's where we'll begin to spread it.

When I arrived for Christmas at Meemaw's house at the low point of my life, she stepped in and saved me by making me feel like I was worth it to change, that I deserved a better life. Ten months later, when I hit the wall during the Denver marathon, my dad did the exact same thing.

"Just push through," he said as his hand grabbed my neck to pull me back onto the road. We had promised to stay together and finish our first marathon as a team. It had become our tradition for every big race. At that point, that promise was the only thing keeping me going. If it weren't for my dad literally pushing me back on track, I would have been sitting on a curb in downtown Denver. I was ready to give up.

But Pa grabbed my collar, and every few feet I felt his hand slap the back of my neck. It was annoying. All I wanted was to stop the race, and here he was, making sure that didn't happen. He dedicated all his energy into standing in my way of quitting. I begged him to let me sit down, to let me stop, but he didn't. We scratched and clawed our way on, and 6.2 miles later we crossed the finish line with our hands in the air. Volunteers hung our finisher's medals around our necks and it was official—we were marathoners. Life would never really be the same.

And as the weight of the medal hung on my chest, I realized the wall, and everything after, had become a metaphor for this entire journey. As cheesy as it was, it really summed up the whole thing.

There are going to be so many times when you want to give up—that the weight of reaching your goals and dreams becomes too much. There are going to be times when you want to run to the curb and sit down as everyone else passes you by. When it happens, you're going to need someone to reach out, grab your neck and pull you back. Someone to say, "No. We're sticking with it. It sucks now, but we're pushing through." And there are going to be so many times when the people that you love and that you care about are going to need you to do the same. Grab their neck and tell them to keep running, literally or otherwise. *This* is what it's all about. Doing these things, and doing them together. Running the miles and sharing the smiles.

And it's not always going to be easy. Very rarely, in fact, is it going to be easy. But it's always, *always*, going to be worth it.

Reader Testimonial

Do Life changed my life and, in turn, the lives of the teens and adults around me. This is a true pay-it-forward movement. My husband and I are house parents at a boarding school for youth in at-risk situations. Many of these teens have weight issues. The school decided that it was a priority to help them get fit. I knew that I could not tell them to do something that I myself wasn't willing to do. My sister handed me a copy of Runner's World *with Ben's story in it, and I was inspired!*

Do Life became the support I needed to change my life so that I could, in turn, influence those around me. So far, I've lost twenty-three pounds and coached about fifty kids and adults in a C25K ("Couch to 5K") program. Our "race" is Wednesday and 185 students and staff members will be participating. I've also committed to running four half marathons and a minimum of one 5K per month, including a warrior dash. Next, I'm going to go for the marathon. Ben, I cannot thank you enough for changing my life so that I can help others do the same thing! —Arlene S

running glossary

BANDIT: Someone who runs a race without paying the entry fee/qualifying for the race. Banditing is more or less frowned upon.

BONK: The moment when everything that can go wrong during a run or race does go wrong. This is also known as "hitting the wall." A bonkee will break down physically and mentally from exhaustion and might not finish the race at all. Every runner will experience a bonk in his or her lifetime.

DFL: Dead fucking last. This is something of a badge of honor. No matter what, someone has to come in last, and these champions are the ones who tough it out the longest.

DNF: Did not finish. The official race result for people who start a race but don't finish.

DNS: Did not start. The official race result for people who signed up for a race, but didn't, for one reason or another, make it to the starting line or dropped out just before the race.

FARTLEKS: Perhaps the most fun word in all of running, fartlek is a mix of steady and tempo pacing during your run in an effort to increase overall speed. Fartleks also help push your heart rate up—something that standard easy runs don't necessarily do. An example of a fartlek run is a five-mile run with sixty-second sprints every five minutes.

FUEL BELT: Some runners choose to wear fancy hydration and fuel belts that you can find at any running store. The belt allows you to carry your own water bottles and gel packs with you.

GPS WATCH: A great training device, usually in the form of a Garmin Forerunner or Polar GPS watch. It keeps up with your distance, pace, and even heart rate for optimal training tracking. You'll have to spend a little money for the luxury, but it's well worth it if you're going to be training regularly.

HEEL STRIKE: A common improper running form when the runner lands each stride heel-first and rolls to the toe. Proper form is to land in the middle of the foot, absorbing the impact over a larger area, and thus lessening the chance of injury.

HILL REPEATS: Like intervals, repeating hills with set rests or walk breaks in between. Find a nice quarter-mile hill for your repeats.

INTERVALS: Predetermined repeats of set distances. Most often, these are run at a fast pace with a set rest/walk period in between each set. Example: eight-by-four-hundred-meters with a sixty-second break between each set.

KICK: The last meters of the race when a runner will dramatically increase speed to pass someone, maintain a lead, break a PR, or beat a personal goal.

NEGATIVE SPLITS: Running the second half of a race faster than the first half. Negative splitting takes discipline, but is the recipe for faster runs. Our instinct is to start too quickly and burn out. Save some energy, earn negative splits, and be pleasantly surprised as your times get better.

PR: Personal record. Most runners are racing against themselves, so it's important to keep up with your PRs regardless of speed or distance.

PRONATION: The runner's natural foot roll (inside, outside, or midfoot). Pronation is important in determining proper shoes, so go to your local running store to get your pronation checked.

RICE: The RICE method stands for Rest, Ice, Compress, and Elevate—the four most important things about recovery and injury prevention.

SPEED WORK: Training that is designed to make you a *faster* runner. This encompasses a variety of workouts, but is most typically done in the form of intervals (see above).

RUNNING GLOSSARY

25-week runner's journal

tHE RUNNING JOURNAL is an important part of the runner's (of all abilities) life. I've found that logging each and every mile is not only helpful for training but infinitely satisfying to look back on in six months, a year, or even three.

This logbook is for you to track your miles, but also to give you an idea of the progress you're making as you train your way through the weeks, whether it be toward your first 5K, your tenth marathon, or even if you're just running for fun.

Also included is a nutrition diary for if you're tracking your meals.

DAY ONE, DATE:

Miles _____ Time _____

Weather _____

Terrain _____

Notes _____

_____

_____

Breakfast _____

Lunch _____

Dinner _____

Snacks _____

DAY TWO, DATE:

Miles _____ Time _____

Weather _____

Terrain _____

Notes _____

_____

_____

Breakfast _____

Lunch _____

Dinner _____

Snacks _____

DAY THREE, DATE:

Miles _____ Time _____

Weather _____

Terrain _____

Notes _____

_____

_____

Breakfast _____

Lunch _____

Dinner _____

Snacks _____

DAY FOUR, DATE:

Miles _____ Time _____

Weather _____

Terrain _____

Notes _____

_____

_____

Breakfast _____

Lunch _____

Dinner _____

Snacks _____

DAY FIVE, DATE:

Miles _____ Time _____

Weather _____

Terrain _____

Notes _____

_____

_____

Breakfast _____

Lunch _____

Dinner _____

Snacks _____

DAY SIX, DATE:

Miles _____ Time _____

Weather _____

Terrain _____

Notes _____

_____

_____

Breakfast _____

Lunch _____

Dinner _____

Snacks _____

DAY SEVEN, DATE:

Miles _____ Time _____

Weather _____

Terrain _____

Notes _____

_____

_____

Breakfast _____

Lunch _____

Dinner _____

Snacks _____

week one

DAY ONE, DATE:

Miles _____ Time _____

Weather _____

Terrain _____

Notes _____

_____

_____

Breakfast _____

Lunch _____

Dinner _____

Snacks _____

DAY TWO, DATE:

Miles _____ Time _____

Weather _____

Terrain _____

Notes _____

_____

_____

Breakfast _____

Lunch _____

Dinner _____

Snacks _____

DAY THREE, DATE:

Miles _____ Time _____

Weather _____

Terrain _____

Notes _____

_____

_____

Breakfast _____

Lunch _____

Dinner _____

Snacks _____

DAY FOUR, DATE:

Miles _____ Time _____

Weather _____

Terrain _____

Notes _____

_____

_____

Breakfast _____

Lunch _____

Dinner _____

Snacks _____

week two

DAY FIVE, DATE:

Miles _____ Time _____

Weather _____

Terrain _____

Notes _____

_____

_____

Breakfast _____

Lunch _____

Dinner _____

Snacks _____

DAY SIX, DATE:

Miles _____ Time _____

Weather _____

Terrain _____

Notes _____

_____

_____

Breakfast _____

Lunch _____

Dinner _____

Snacks _____

DAY SEVEN, DATE:

Miles _____ Time _____

Weather _____

Terrain _____

Notes _____

_____

_____

Breakfast _____

Lunch _____

Dinner _____

Snacks _____

week two

DAY ONE, DATE:

Miles _____ Time _____

Weather _____

Terrain _____

Notes _____

_____

_____

Breakfast _____

Lunch _____

Dinner _____

Snacks _____

DAY TWO, DATE:

Miles _____ Time _____

Weather _____

Terrain _____

Notes _____

_____

_____

Breakfast _____

Lunch _____

Dinner _____

Snacks _____

DAY THREE, DATE:

Miles _____ Time _____

Weather _____

Terrain _____

Notes _____

_____

_____

Breakfast _____

Lunch _____

Dinner _____

Snacks _____

DAY FOUR, DATE:

Miles _____ Time _____

Weather _____

Terrain _____

Notes _____

_____

_____

Breakfast _____

Lunch _____

Dinner _____

Snacks _____

week three

DAY FIVE, DATE:

Miles _____ Time _____

Weather _____

Terrain _____

Notes _____

_____

_____

Breakfast _____

Lunch _____

Dinner _____

Snacks _____

DAY SIX, DATE:

Miles _____ Time _____

Weather _____

Terrain _____

Notes _____

_____

_____

Breakfast _____

Lunch _____

Dinner _____

Snacks _____

DAY SEVEN, DATE:

Miles _____ Time _____

Weather _____

Terrain _____

Notes _____

_____

_____

Breakfast _____

Lunch _____

Dinner _____

Snacks _____

DAY ONE, DATE:

Miles _____ Time _____

Weather _____

Terrain _____

Notes _____

_____

_____

Breakfast _____

Lunch _____

Dinner _____

Snacks _____

DAY TWO, DATE:

Miles _____ Time _____

Weather _____

Terrain _____

Notes _____

_____

_____

Breakfast _____

Lunch _____

Dinner _____

Snacks _____

DAY THREE, DATE:

Miles _____ Time _____

Weather _____

Terrain _____

Notes _____

_____

_____

Breakfast _____

Lunch _____

Dinner _____

Snacks _____

DAY FOUR, DATE:

Miles _____ Time _____

Weather _____

Terrain _____

Notes _____

_____

_____

Breakfast _____

Lunch _____

Dinner _____

Snacks _____

week four

DAY FIVE, DATE:

Miles _____ Time _____

Weather _____

Terrain _____

Notes _____

_____

_____

Breakfast _____

Lunch _____

Dinner _____

Snacks _____

DAY SIX, DATE:

Miles _____ Time _____

Weather _____

Terrain _____

Notes _____

_____

_____

Breakfast _____

Lunch _____

Dinner _____

Snacks _____

DAY SEVEN, DATE:

Miles _____ Time _____

Weather _____

Terrain _____

Notes _____

_____

_____

Breakfast _____

Lunch _____

Dinner _____

Snacks _____

week four

DAY ONE, DATE:

Miles _____ Time _____

Weather _____

Terrain _____

Notes _____

_____

_____

Breakfast _____

Lunch _____

Dinner _____

Snacks _____

DAY TWO, DATE:

Miles _____ Time _____

Weather _____

Terrain _____

Notes _____

_____

_____

Breakfast _____

Lunch _____

Dinner _____

Snacks _____

DAY THREE, DATE:

Miles _____ Time _____

Weather _____

Terrain _____

Notes _____

_____

_____

Breakfast _____

Lunch _____

Dinner _____

Snacks _____

DAY FOUR, DATE:

Miles _____ Time _____

Weather _____

Terrain _____

Notes _____

_____

_____

Breakfast _____

Lunch _____

Dinner _____

Snacks _____

week five

DAY FIVE, DATE:

Miles _____ Time _____

Weather _____

Terrain _____

Notes _____

_____

_____

Breakfast _____

Lunch _____

Dinner _____

Snacks _____

DAY SIX, DATE:

Miles _____ Time _____

Weather _____

Terrain _____

Notes _____

_____

_____

Breakfast _____

Lunch _____

Dinner _____

Snacks _____

DAY SEVEN, DATE:

Miles _____ Time _____

Weather _____

Terrain _____

Notes _____

_____

_____

Breakfast _____

Lunch _____

Dinner _____

Snacks _____

DAY ONE, DATE:

Miles _____ Time _____

Weather _____

Terrain _____

Notes _____

_____

_____

Breakfast _____

Lunch _____

Dinner _____

Snacks _____

DAY TWO, DATE:

Miles _____ Time _____

Weather _____

Terrain _____

Notes _____

_____

_____

Breakfast _____

Lunch _____

Dinner _____

Snacks _____

DAY THREE, DATE:

Miles _____ Time _____

Weather _____

Terrain _____

Notes _____

_____

_____

Breakfast _____

Lunch _____

Dinner _____

Snacks _____

DAY FOUR, DATE:

Miles _____ Time _____

Weather _____

Terrain _____

Notes _____

_____

_____

Breakfast _____

Lunch _____

Dinner _____

Snacks _____

week six

DAY FIVE, DATE:

Miles _____ Time _____

Weather _____

Terrain _____

Notes _____

_____

_____

Breakfast _____

Lunch _____

Dinner _____

Snacks _____

DAY SIX, DATE:

Miles _____ Time _____

Weather _____

Terrain _____

Notes _____

_____

_____

Breakfast _____

Lunch _____

Dinner _____

Snacks _____

DAY SEVEN, DATE:

Miles _____ Time _____

Weather _____

Terrain _____

Notes _____

_____

_____

Breakfast _____

Lunch _____

Dinner _____

Snacks _____

DAY ONE, DATE:

Miles _____ Time _____

Weather _____

Terrain _____

Notes _____

_____

_____

Breakfast _____

Lunch _____

Dinner _____

Snacks _____

DAY TWO, DATE:

Miles _____ Time _____

Weather _____

Terrain _____

Notes _____

_____

_____

Breakfast _____

Lunch _____

Dinner _____

Snacks _____

DAY THREE, DATE:

Miles _____ Time _____

Weather _____

Terrain _____

Notes _____

_____

_____

Breakfast _____

Lunch _____

Dinner _____

Snacks _____

DAY FOUR, DATE:

Miles _____ Time _____

Weather _____

Terrain _____

Notes _____

_____

_____

Breakfast _____

Lunch _____

Dinner _____

Snacks _____

week seven

DAY FIVE, DATE:

Miles _____ Time _____

Weather _____

Terrain _____

Notes _____

_____

_____

Breakfast _____

Lunch _____

Dinner _____

Snacks _____

DAY SIX, DATE:

Miles _____ Time _____

Weather _____

Terrain _____

Notes _____

_____

_____

Breakfast _____

Lunch _____

Dinner _____

Snacks _____

DAY SEVEN, DATE:

Miles _____ Time _____

Weather _____

Terrain _____

Notes _____

_____

_____

Breakfast _____

Lunch _____

Dinner _____

Snacks _____

week seven

DAY ONE, DATE:

Miles _____ Time _____

Weather _____

Terrain _____

Notes _____

_____

_____

Breakfast _____

Lunch _____

Dinner _____

Snacks _____

DAY TWO, DATE:

Miles _____ Time _____

Weather _____

Terrain _____

Notes _____

_____

_____

Breakfast _____

Lunch _____

Dinner _____

Snacks _____

DAY THREE, DATE:

Miles _____ Time _____

Weather _____

Terrain _____

Notes _____

_____

_____

Breakfast _____

Lunch _____

Dinner _____

Snacks _____

DAY FOUR, DATE:

Miles _____ Time _____

Weather _____

Terrain _____

Notes _____

_____

_____

Breakfast _____

Lunch _____

Dinner _____

Snacks _____

week eight

DAY FIVE, DATE:

Miles _____ Time _____

Weather _____

Terrain _____

Notes _____

_____

_____

Breakfast _____

Lunch _____

Dinner _____

Snacks _____

DAY SIX, DATE:

Miles _____ Time _____

Weather _____

Terrain _____

Notes _____

_____

_____

Breakfast _____

Lunch _____

Dinner _____

Snacks _____

DAY SEVEN, DATE:

Miles _____ Time _____

Weather _____

Terrain _____

Notes _____

_____

_____

Breakfast _____

Lunch _____

Dinner _____

Snacks _____

DAY ONE, DATE:

Miles _____ Time _____

Weather _____

Terrain _____

Notes _____

_____

_____

Breakfast _____

Lunch _____

Dinner _____

Snacks _____

DAY TWO, DATE:

Miles _____ Time _____

Weather _____

Terrain _____

Notes _____

_____

_____

Breakfast _____

Lunch _____

Dinner _____

Snacks _____

DAY THREE, DATE:

Miles _____ Time _____

Weather _____

Terrain _____

Notes _____

_____

_____

Breakfast _____

Lunch _____

Dinner _____

Snacks _____

DAY FOUR, DATE:

Miles _____ Time _____

Weather _____

Terrain _____

Notes _____

_____

_____

Breakfast _____

Lunch _____

Dinner _____

Snacks _____

week nine

DAY FIVE, DATE:

Miles _____ Time _____

Weather _____

Terrain _____

Notes _____

_____

_____

Breakfast _____

Lunch _____

Dinner _____

Snacks _____

DAY SIX, DATE:

Miles _____ Time _____

Weather _____

Terrain _____

Notes _____

_____

_____

Breakfast _____

Lunch _____

Dinner _____

Snacks _____

DAY SEVEN, DATE:

Miles _____ Time _____

Weather _____

Terrain _____

Notes _____

_____

_____

Breakfast _____

Lunch _____

Dinner _____

Snacks _____

DAY ONE, DATE:

Miles _____ Time _____

Weather _____

Terrain _____

Notes _____

_____

_____

Breakfast _____

Lunch _____

Dinner _____

Snacks _____

DAY TWO, DATE:

Miles _____ Time _____

Weather _____

Terrain _____

Notes _____

_____

_____

Breakfast _____

Lunch _____

Dinner _____

Snacks _____

DAY THREE, DATE:

Miles _____ Time _____

Weather _____

Terrain _____

Notes _____

_____

_____

Breakfast _____

Lunch _____

Dinner _____

Snacks _____

DAY FOUR, DATE:

Miles _____ Time _____

Weather _____

Terrain _____

Notes _____

_____

_____

Breakfast _____

Lunch _____

Dinner _____

Snacks _____

week ten

DAY FIVE, DATE:

Miles _____ Time _____

Weather _____

Terrain _____

Notes _____

_____

_____

Breakfast _____

Lunch _____

Dinner _____

Snacks _____

DAY SIX, DATE:

Miles _____ Time _____

Weather _____

Terrain _____

Notes _____

_____

_____

Breakfast _____

Lunch _____

Dinner _____

Snacks _____

DAY SEVEN, DATE:

Miles _____ Time _____

Weather _____

Terrain _____

Notes _____

_____

_____

Breakfast _____

Lunch _____

Dinner _____

Snacks _____

DAY ONE, DATE:

Miles _____ Time _____

Weather _____

Terrain _____

Notes _____

_____

_____

Breakfast _____

Lunch _____

Dinner _____

Snacks _____

DAY TWO, DATE:

Miles _____ Time _____

Weather _____

Terrain _____

Notes _____

_____

_____

Breakfast _____

Lunch _____

Dinner _____

Snacks _____

DAY THREE, DATE:

Miles _____ Time _____

Weather _____

Terrain _____

Notes _____

_____

_____

Breakfast _____

Lunch _____

Dinner _____

Snacks _____

DAY FOUR, DATE:

Miles _____ Time _____

Weather _____

Terrain _____

Notes _____

_____

_____

Breakfast _____

Lunch _____

Dinner _____

Snacks _____

week eleven

DAY FIVE, DATE:

Miles _____ Time _____

Weather _____

Terrain _____

Notes _____

_____

_____

Breakfast _____

Lunch _____

Dinner _____

Snacks _____

DAY SIX, DATE:

Miles _____ Time _____

Weather _____

Terrain _____

Notes _____

_____

_____

Breakfast _____

Lunch _____

Dinner _____

Snacks _____

DAY SEVEN, DATE:

Miles _____ Time _____

Weather _____

Terrain _____

Notes _____

_____

_____

Breakfast _____

Lunch _____

Dinner _____

Snacks _____

week eleven

DAY ONE, DATE:

Miles _____ Time _____

Weather _____

Terrain _____

Notes _____

_____

_____

Breakfast _____

Lunch _____

Dinner _____

Snacks _____

DAY TWO, DATE:

Miles _____ Time _____

Weather _____

Terrain _____

Notes _____

_____

_____

Breakfast _____

Lunch _____

Dinner _____

Snacks _____

DAY THREE, DATE:

Miles _____ Time _____

Weather _____

Terrain _____

Notes _____

_____

_____

Breakfast _____

Lunch _____

Dinner _____

Snacks _____

DAY FOUR, DATE:

Miles _____ Time _____

Weather _____

Terrain _____

Notes _____

_____

_____

Breakfast _____

Lunch _____

Dinner _____

Snacks _____

week twelve

DAY FIVE, DATE:

Miles _____ Time _____

Weather _____

Terrain _____

Notes _____

_____

_____

Breakfast _____

Lunch _____

Dinner _____

Snacks _____

DAY SIX, DATE:

Miles _____ Time _____

Weather _____

Terrain _____

Notes _____

_____

_____

Breakfast _____

Lunch _____

Dinner _____

Snacks _____

DAY SEVEN, DATE:

Miles _____ Time _____

Weather _____

Terrain _____

Notes _____

_____

_____

Breakfast _____

Lunch _____

Dinner _____

Snacks _____

DAY ONE, DATE:

Miles _____ Time _____

Weather _____

Terrain _____

Notes _____

_____

_____

Breakfast _____

Lunch _____

Dinner _____

Snacks _____

DAY TWO, DATE:

Miles _____ Time _____

Weather _____

Terrain _____

Notes _____

_____

_____

Breakfast _____

Lunch _____

Dinner _____

Snacks _____

DAY THREE, DATE:

Miles _____ Time _____

Weather _____

Terrain _____

Notes _____

_____

_____

Breakfast _____

Lunch _____

Dinner _____

Snacks _____

DAY FOUR, DATE:

Miles _____ Time _____

Weather _____

Terrain _____

Notes _____

_____

_____

Breakfast _____

Lunch _____

Dinner _____

Snacks _____

week thirteen

DAY FIVE, DATE:

Miles _____ Time _____

Weather _____

Terrain _____

Notes _____

_____

_____

Breakfast _____

Lunch _____

Dinner _____

Snacks _____

DAY SIX, DATE:

Miles _____ Time _____

Weather _____

Terrain _____

Notes _____

_____

_____

Breakfast _____

Lunch _____

Dinner _____

Snacks _____

DAY SEVEN, DATE:

Miles _____ Time _____

Weather _____

Terrain _____

Notes _____

_____

_____

Breakfast _____

Lunch _____

Dinner _____

Snacks _____

week thirteen

DAY ONE, DATE:

Miles _____ Time _____

Weather _____

Terrain _____

Notes _____

_____

_____

Breakfast _____

Lunch _____

Dinner _____

Snacks _____

DAY TWO, DATE:

Miles _____ Time _____

Weather _____

Terrain _____

Notes _____

_____

_____

Breakfast _____

Lunch _____

Dinner _____

Snacks _____

DAY THREE, DATE:

Miles _____ Time _____

Weather _____

Terrain _____

Notes _____

_____

_____

Breakfast _____

Lunch _____

Dinner _____

Snacks _____

DAY FOUR, DATE:

Miles _____ Time _____

Weather _____

Terrain _____

Notes _____

_____

_____

Breakfast _____

Lunch _____

Dinner _____

Snacks _____

week fourteen

DAY FIVE, DATE:

Miles _____ Time _____

Weather _____

Terrain _____

Notes _____

_____

_____

Breakfast _____

Lunch _____

Dinner _____

Snacks _____

DAY SIX, DATE:

Miles _____ Time _____

Weather _____

Terrain _____

Notes _____

_____

_____

Breakfast _____

Lunch _____

Dinner _____

Snacks _____

DAY SEVEN, DATE:

Miles _____ Time _____

Weather _____

Terrain _____

Notes _____

_____

_____

Breakfast _____

Lunch _____

Dinner _____

Snacks _____

DAY ONE, DATE:

Miles _____ Time _____

Weather _____

Terrain _____

Notes _____

_____

_____

Breakfast _____

Lunch _____

Dinner _____

Snacks _____

DAY TWO, DATE:

Miles _____ Time _____

Weather _____

Terrain _____

Notes _____

_____

_____

Breakfast _____

Lunch _____

Dinner _____

Snacks _____

DAY THREE, DATE:

Miles _____ Time _____

Weather _____

Terrain _____

Notes _____

_____

_____

Breakfast _____

Lunch _____

Dinner _____

Snacks _____

DAY FOUR, DATE:

Miles _____ Time _____

Weather _____

Terrain _____

Notes _____

_____

_____

Breakfast _____

Lunch _____

Dinner _____

Snacks _____

week fifteen

DAY FIVE, DATE:

Miles _____ Time _____

Weather _____

Terrain _____

Notes _____

_____

_____

Breakfast _____

Lunch _____

Dinner _____

Snacks _____

DAY SIX, DATE:

Miles _____ Time _____

Weather _____

Terrain _____

Notes _____

_____

_____

Breakfast _____

Lunch _____

Dinner _____

Snacks _____

DAY SEVEN, DATE:

Miles _____ Time _____

Weather _____

Terrain _____

Notes _____

_____

_____

Breakfast _____

Lunch _____

Dinner _____

Snacks _____

week fifteen

DAY ONE, DATE:

Miles _____ Time _____

Weather _____

Terrain _____

Notes _____

_____

_____

Breakfast _____

Lunch _____

Dinner _____

Snacks _____

DAY TWO, DATE:

Miles _____ Time _____

Weather _____

Terrain _____

Notes _____

_____

_____

Breakfast _____

Lunch _____

Dinner _____

Snacks _____

DAY THREE, DATE:

Miles _____ Time _____

Weather _____

Terrain _____

Notes _____

_____

_____

Breakfast _____

Lunch _____

Dinner _____

Snacks _____

DAY FOUR, DATE:

Miles _____ Time _____

Weather _____

Terrain _____

Notes _____

_____

_____

Breakfast _____

Lunch _____

Dinner _____

Snacks _____

week sixteen

DAY FIVE, DATE:

Miles _____ Time _____

Weather _____

Terrain _____

Notes _____

_____

_____

Breakfast _____

Lunch _____

Dinner _____

Snacks _____

DAY SIX, DATE:

Miles _____ Time _____

Weather _____

Terrain _____

Notes _____

_____

_____

Breakfast _____

Lunch _____

Dinner _____

Snacks _____

DAY SEVEN, DATE:

Miles _____ Time _____

Weather _____

Terrain _____

Notes _____

_____

_____

Breakfast _____

Lunch _____

Dinner _____

Snacks _____

DAY ONE, DATE:

Miles _____ Time _____

Weather _____

Terrain _____

Notes _____

_____

_____

Breakfast _____

Lunch _____

Dinner _____

Snacks _____

DAY TWO, DATE:

Miles _____ Time _____

Weather _____

Terrain _____

Notes _____

_____

_____

Breakfast _____

Lunch _____

Dinner _____

Snacks _____

DAY THREE, DATE:

Miles _____ Time _____

Weather _____

Terrain _____

Notes _____

_____

_____

Breakfast _____

Lunch _____

Dinner _____

Snacks _____

DAY FOUR, DATE:

Miles _____ Time _____

Weather _____

Terrain _____

Notes _____

_____

_____

Breakfast _____

Lunch _____

Dinner _____

Snacks _____

week seventeen

DAY FIVE, DATE:

Miles _____ Time _____

Weather _____

Terrain _____

Notes _____

_____

_____

Breakfast _____

Lunch _____

Dinner _____

Snacks _____

DAY SIX, DATE:

Miles _____ Time _____

Weather _____

Terrain _____

Notes _____

_____

_____

Breakfast _____

Lunch _____

Dinner _____

Snacks _____

DAY SEVEN, DATE:

Miles _____ Time _____

Weather _____

Terrain _____

Notes _____

_____

_____

Breakfast _____

Lunch _____

Dinner _____

Snacks _____

DAY ONE, DATE:

Miles _____ Time _____

Weather _____

Terrain _____

Notes _____

_____

_____

Breakfast _____

Lunch _____

Dinner _____

Snacks _____

DAY TWO, DATE:

Miles _____ Time _____

Weather _____

Terrain _____

Notes _____

_____

_____

Breakfast _____

Lunch _____

Dinner _____

Snacks _____

DAY THREE, DATE:

Miles _____ Time _____

Weather _____

Terrain _____

Notes _____

_____

_____

Breakfast _____

Lunch _____

Dinner _____

Snacks _____

DAY FOUR, DATE:

Miles _____ Time _____

Weather _____

Terrain _____

Notes _____

_____

_____

Breakfast _____

Lunch _____

Dinner _____

Snacks _____

week eighteen

DAY FIVE, DATE:

Miles _____ Time _____

Weather _____

Terrain _____

Notes _____

_____

_____

Breakfast _____

Lunch _____

Dinner _____

Snacks _____

DAY SIX, DATE:

Miles _____ Time _____

Weather _____

Terrain _____

Notes _____

_____

_____

Breakfast _____

Lunch _____

Dinner _____

Snacks _____

DAY SEVEN, DATE:

Miles _____ Time _____

Weather _____

Terrain _____

Notes _____

_____

_____

Breakfast _____

Lunch _____

Dinner _____

Snacks _____

week eighteen

DAY ONE, DATE:

Miles _____ Time _____

Weather _____

Terrain _____

Notes _____

_____

_____

Breakfast _____

Lunch _____

Dinner _____

Snacks _____

DAY TWO, DATE:

Miles _____ Time _____

Weather _____

Terrain _____

Notes _____

_____

_____

Breakfast _____

Lunch _____

Dinner _____

Snacks _____

DAY THREE, DATE:

Miles _____ Time _____

Weather _____

Terrain _____

Notes _____

_____

_____

Breakfast _____

Lunch _____

Dinner _____

Snacks _____

DAY FOUR, DATE:

Miles _____ Time _____

Weather _____

Terrain _____

Notes _____

_____

_____

Breakfast _____

Lunch _____

Dinner _____

Snacks _____

week nineteen

DAY FIVE, DATE:

Miles _____ Time _____

Weather _____

Terrain _____

Notes _____

_____

_____

Breakfast _____

Lunch _____

Dinner _____

Snacks _____

DAY SIX, DATE:

Miles _____ Time _____

Weather _____

Terrain _____

Notes _____

_____

_____

Breakfast _____

Lunch _____

Dinner _____

Snacks _____

DAY SEVEN, DATE:

Miles _____ Time _____

Weather _____

Terrain _____

Notes _____

_____

_____

Breakfast _____

Lunch _____

Dinner _____

Snacks _____

week nineteen

DAY ONE, DATE:

Miles _____ Time _____

Weather _____

Terrain _____

Notes _____

_____

_____

Breakfast _____

Lunch _____

Dinner _____

Snacks _____

DAY TWO, DATE:

Miles _____ Time _____

Weather _____

Terrain _____

Notes _____

_____

_____

Breakfast _____

Lunch _____

Dinner _____

Snacks _____

DAY THREE, DATE:

Miles _____ Time _____

Weather _____

Terrain _____

Notes _____

_____

_____

Breakfast _____

Lunch _____

Dinner _____

Snacks _____

DAY FOUR, DATE:

Miles _____ Time _____

Weather _____

Terrain _____

Notes _____

_____

_____

Breakfast _____

Lunch _____

Dinner _____

Snacks _____

week twenty

DAY FIVE, DATE:

Miles _____ Time _____

Weather _____

Terrain _____

Notes _____

_____

_____

Breakfast _____

Lunch _____

Dinner _____

Snacks _____

DAY SIX, DATE:

Miles _____ Time _____

Weather _____

Terrain _____

Notes _____

_____

_____

Breakfast _____

Lunch _____

Dinner _____

Snacks _____

DAY SEVEN, DATE:

Miles _____ Time _____

Weather _____

Terrain _____

Notes _____

_____

_____

Breakfast _____

Lunch _____

Dinner _____

Snacks _____

DAY ONE, DATE:

Miles _____ Time _____

Weather _____

Terrain _____

Notes _____

_____

_____

Breakfast _____

Lunch _____

Dinner _____

Snacks _____

DAY TWO, DATE:

Miles _____ Time _____

Weather _____

Terrain _____

Notes _____

_____

_____

Breakfast _____

Lunch _____

Dinner _____

Snacks _____

DAY THREE, DATE:

Miles _____ Time _____

Weather _____

Terrain _____

Notes _____

_____

_____

Breakfast _____

Lunch _____

Dinner _____

Snacks _____

DAY FOUR, DATE:

Miles _____ Time _____

Weather _____

Terrain _____

Notes _____

_____

_____

Breakfast _____

Lunch _____

Dinner _____

Snacks _____

week twenty-one

DAY FIVE, DATE:

Miles _____ Time _____

Weather _____

Terrain _____

Notes _____

_____

_____

Breakfast _____

Lunch _____

Dinner _____

Snacks _____

DAY SIX, DATE:

Miles _____ Time _____

Weather _____

Terrain _____

Notes _____

_____

_____

Breakfast _____

Lunch _____

Dinner _____

Snacks _____

DAY SEVEN, DATE:

Miles _____ Time _____

Weather _____

Terrain _____

Notes _____

_____

_____

Breakfast _____

Lunch _____

Dinner _____

Snacks _____

DAY ONE, DATE:

Miles _____ Time _____

Weather _____

Terrain _____

Notes _____

_____

_____

Breakfast _____

Lunch _____

Dinner _____

Snacks _____

DAY TWO, DATE:

Miles _____ Time _____

Weather _____

Terrain _____

Notes _____

_____

_____

Breakfast _____

Lunch _____

Dinner _____

Snacks _____

DAY THREE, DATE:

Miles _____ Time _____

Weather _____

Terrain _____

Notes _____

_____

_____

Breakfast _____

Lunch _____

Dinner _____

Snacks _____

DAY FOUR, DATE:

Miles _____ Time _____

Weather _____

Terrain _____

Notes _____

_____

_____

Breakfast _____

Lunch _____

Dinner _____

Snacks _____

week twenty-two

DAY FIVE, DATE:

Miles _____ Time _____

Weather _____

Terrain _____

Notes _____

_____

_____

Breakfast _____

Lunch _____

Dinner _____

Snacks _____

DAY SIX, DATE:

Miles _____ Time _____

Weather _____

Terrain _____

Notes _____

_____

_____

Breakfast _____

Lunch _____

Dinner _____

Snacks _____

DAY SEVEN, DATE:

Miles _____ Time _____

Weather _____

Terrain _____

Notes _____

_____

_____

Breakfast _____

Lunch _____

Dinner _____

Snacks _____

DAY ONE, DATE:

Miles _____ Time _____

Weather _____

Terrain _____

Notes _____

_____

_____

Breakfast _____

Lunch _____

Dinner _____

Snacks _____

DAY TWO, DATE:

Miles _____ Time _____

Weather _____

Terrain _____

Notes _____

_____

_____

Breakfast _____

Lunch _____

Dinner _____

Snacks _____

DAY THREE, DATE:

Miles _____ Time _____

Weather _____

Terrain _____

Notes _____

_____

_____

Breakfast _____

Lunch _____

Dinner _____

Snacks _____

DAY FOUR, DATE:

Miles _____ Time _____

Weather _____

Terrain _____

Notes _____

_____

_____

Breakfast _____

Lunch _____

Dinner _____

Snacks _____

week twenty-three

DAY FIVE, DATE:

Miles _____ Time _____

Weather _____

Terrain _____

Notes _____

_____

_____

Breakfast _____

Lunch _____

Dinner _____

Snacks _____

DAY SIX, DATE:

Miles _____ Time _____

Weather _____

Terrain _____

Notes _____

_____

_____

Breakfast _____

Lunch _____

Dinner _____

Snacks _____

DAY SEVEN, DATE:

Miles _____ Time _____

Weather _____

Terrain _____

Notes _____

_____

_____

Breakfast _____

Lunch _____

Dinner _____

Snacks _____

Week twenty-three

DAY ONE, DATE:

Miles _____ Time _____

Weather _____

Terrain _____

Notes _____

_____

_____

Breakfast _____

Lunch _____

Dinner _____

Snacks _____

DAY TWO, DATE:

Miles _____ Time _____

Weather _____

Terrain _____

Notes _____

_____

_____

Breakfast _____

Lunch _____

Dinner _____

Snacks _____

DAY THREE, DATE:

Miles _____ Time _____

Weather _____

Terrain _____

Notes _____

_____

_____

Breakfast _____

Lunch _____

Dinner _____

Snacks _____

DAY FOUR, DATE:

Miles _____ Time _____

Weather _____

Terrain _____

Notes _____

_____

_____

Breakfast _____

Lunch _____

Dinner _____

Snacks _____

week twenty-four

DAY FIVE, DATE:

Miles _____ Time _____

Weather _____

Terrain _____

Notes _____

_____

_____

Breakfast _____

Lunch _____

Dinner _____

Snacks _____

DAY SIX, DATE:

Miles _____ Time _____

Weather _____

Terrain _____

Notes _____

_____

_____

Breakfast _____

Lunch _____

Dinner _____

Snacks _____

DAY SEVEN, DATE:

Miles _____ Time _____

Weather _____

Terrain _____

Notes _____

_____

_____

Breakfast _____

Lunch _____

Dinner _____

Snacks _____

DAY ONE, DATE:

Miles _____ Time _____

Weather _____

Terrain _____

Notes _____

_____

_____

Breakfast _____

Lunch _____

Dinner _____

Snacks _____

DAY TWO, DATE:

Miles _____ Time _____

Weather _____

Terrain _____

Notes _____

_____

_____

Breakfast _____

Lunch _____

Dinner _____

Snacks _____

DAY THREE, DATE:

Miles _____ Time _____

Weather _____

Terrain _____

Notes _____

_____

_____

Breakfast _____

Lunch _____

Dinner _____

Snacks _____

DAY FOUR, DATE:

Miles _____ Time _____

Weather _____

Terrain _____

Notes _____

_____

_____

Breakfast _____

Lunch _____

Dinner _____

Snacks _____

week twenty-five

DAY FIVE, DATE:

Miles _____ Time _____

Weather _____

Terrain _____

Notes _____

_____

_____

Breakfast _____

Lunch _____

Dinner _____

Snacks _____

DAY SIX, DATE:

Miles _____ Time _____

Weather _____

Terrain _____

Notes _____

_____

_____

Breakfast _____

Lunch _____

Dinner _____

Snacks _____

DAY SEVEN, DATE:

Miles _____ Time _____

Weather _____

Terrain _____

Notes _____

_____

_____

Breakfast _____

Lunch _____

Dinner _____

Snacks _____

resources

a **FEW MONTHS AGO,** after a speaking engagement at a university, a young woman approached me and the first thing I noticed was her eyes. They were the eyes of someone who, to put it frankly, had lost hope. I've met quite a few people who were down and trying to find a spark or some motivation, but this girl just looked beaten down by life.

We talked for a few minutes; she confided that she had been sad for years and didn't know where to turn.

I tried my best to help her, knowing how she felt, but was having trouble articulating concrete advice or specific resources that she could investigate.

My main advice is and always has been "join a team to help with the journey," and "find a support system," but when it came down to actual organizations I was drawing a blank, so I decided to do some research.

The important thing to understand is that no matter what the issue you're facing, there are countless organizations, big and small, that you can join—teammates with whom you can share the journey.

This is a sampling of such groups and resources, and I encourage you to check them out, but also look for yourself online since you'll know exactly what you're looking for. The bottom line, though, is that you'll never have enough help when taking on life.

RUNNING

DoLifeMovement.com: I'd be the worst employee ever if I started this list with anything but our own online running/fitness community. There are currently more than two thousand members (which puts us on the smaller, more intimate side) in the community—people embarking on all sorts of life-changing voyages. For the most part, we share a love of running and enjoying it together. We also have local sections where people converse with Do Lifers nearby, organizing meet-ups and sharing local running routes and ideas.

Active.com/Couch-to-5K: A very vibrant and helpful community, Active.com will point you to local races, and the forums at Couch-to-5K will help you on your journey no matter what level runner you are.

Runner's World: I cannot brag about this publication enough, and I wish I'd had known about it when I first started. *Runner's World* is the holy grail of running literature and will give you an incredible wealth of knowledge when starting or continuing your running career. The *Runner's World* Web site (runnersworld.com) also has a great message board to discuss running with other *Runner's World* readers.

DIET

Spark People: SparkPeople.com is the largest online diet and nutrition community with more than twelve million users. I've heard from countless people that the communities on Spark People helped spur them on to lose anywhere from ten to two hundred pounds.

Weight Watchers: Both online and offline, Weight Watchers has a proven track record of not only helping people lose weight, but helping them become much smarter eaters.

Overeaters Anonymous: I highly suggest twelve-step programs to help with any sort of addiction. If food is your addiction, consider OA. You can find more information about this and other twelve-step programs at OA.org.

Local Support Groups: Go to your local health and fitness center and ask about weight-management classes; you'll find that most larger clubs will have regular classes. More often than not, the classes will be headed by a registered dietician.

DEPRESSION

Daily Strength: An online depression support group/ community. You can find out more at DailyStrength .com.

To Write Love on Her Arms: TWLOHA is a nonprofit organization with local chapters at many universities around the country raising suicide awareness and spreading the message of hope.

1-800-SUICIDE: A depression and suicide hotline.

ADDICTION

Narcotics Anonymous: NA.org
Alcoholics Anonymous: AA.org
Gamblers Anonymous: gamblersanonymous.org

acknowledgments

THERE ARE SO many people I need to thank in regards to both this book and the support they have shown throughout this whole process of getting my life together.

First and foremost, Meemaw. Thanks for always being there for me and not being afraid to nudge me to do better in all facets of life.

Jed and Pa, for being there in the very beginning and throughout every step of this whole deal. For being on the team and putting up with my shenanigans over the last few years. For helping in every way possible and holding me accountable.

Thanks to my wonderful fiancée, Brooke, for putting up with my late-night writing marathons, cheering me to dozens of finish lines, and taking care of our neurotic dog, Sherman, when I'm away. Thank you for pushing me out of bed to run even when it's the last thing I want to do.

Mom. You know how much you mean to me. Thanks for everything you've ever given me and for letting me sleep on your floor when I was too scared to sleep alone.

Thanks to my sister, Laura, for showing me that no matter

how tough life is sometimes, everything is better when you can laugh about it.

I have to thank my professors Dr. Francie Bolter, Mark Spitzer, and David Keith. Not only did you teach me how to write effectively (I hope) but you put up with my less than enthusiastic attitudes toward homework and class-attendance policies for three straight years. I appreciate your patience more than you know.

Thanks, in no particular order, to my friends who have run with me and kicked my tail into shape over the years: Heather Hawkins, Charlie Burnett, Michael Miller, Wig, Guy, John, Megan and Blake Hanna, Lee Ann and Laura King.

To the Internet, the Tumblr community, and the folks who have supported the Do Life Movement with the same passion we have. You mean the world to me; thank you for sticking with me through five-thousand-plus blog posts, including, but not limited to, shirtless pictures, bloody-nipple pictures, and missing-toenail pictures.

And last but not least, thanks to the crew at Penguin and New American Library for going above and beyond throughout this writing journey. My editors, Mark Chait and Talia Platz—I couldn't have done it without you. My agent, Chris Park, who has smiled and worked tirelessly through countless headaches as I scrambled to hit the deadlines. Jodi Lipper, for all your hard work and talent and for helping create order where there once was chaos.

I am inexplicably lucky to call you all friends and family.